Acknowledgments

If it takes a village to raise a child, it takes a global network to write a curriculum such as this. Hundreds of individuals and many organizations contributed to *Speaking Out* over the five years of its gestation. We want to pay special tribute to Linda Hawkin Israel, Director of MAMAs, who played a vital role in bringing many of the key participants together and Angela Burke, a graduate student at Portland State University, who participated in the development and writing of the curriculum. The Northwest Sierra Leone Association in Portland, Oregon, also has been a stalwart supporter throughout. Special mention goes to Association members Cecilia Bangura, Emma Fofonah, and Karifa Koroma who served as consultants. Fatima Jarieu Bona and Jariatu Sesay of the Sierra Leone Women's Movement for Peace, New Jersey Branch, also contributed ideas and materials. Thanks also to Zainab Bangura, Sister Catherine Dauda, Corinne Dufka, Haja Dukuray, Bondu Mani, Susan McKay, Yatta Samah, and Susan Shepler for sharing their insights on the Sierra Leonean civil war. Many of their contributions are included as interviews featured in *Speaking Out*.

A number of teachers and academic institutions nurtured this project as it developed from a documentary video to a multi-media curriculum guide. Curriculum specialists Bill Bigelow, Sandra Childs, and Jeff Edmundson served as consultants, and Don Gavitte and Jeffer Daykin assisted by piloting materials in their classrooms. We also want to thank Thomas Becker for contributing an essay and editorial assistance, and Elaine Hays, Jonah Loeb, and PC Peri for technical assistance. Portland State University funded portions of *Speaking Out* through student research grants and a faculty development grant. We also want to express our gratitude to the many students in the Department of Psychology at Portland State University who helped organize conference and community events related to the development of the curriculum.

Students and faculty in the book publication graduate program at Portland State University hold a special place of affection in our hearts for launching this curriculum. Their thoughtful feedback on an earlier version of the guide allowed us to move forward toward this final draft. We want to recognize Dennis Stovall, Bernadette Baker, Peggy Lindquist, Gretchen Stelter, and Paulette Rees-Denis for editing, and Christopher Ross for graphic design work. We also want to pay special tribute to Alan Anderson-Priddy, who contributed countless hours re-editing *Diamonds, Guns, and Rice* as well as editing new special features and designing the DVD.

We are delighted to be publishing *Speaking Out* on the tenth anniversary of the United Nations Fourth World Conference on Women in Beijing. The Platform for Action that grew out of the Beijing conference provided an important source of inspiration for the curriculum.

Speaking Out is dedicated to the many women and men working across the globe, often with limited resources and under trying conditions, to create a more just and equitable world.

J.H.

Contents

SPEAKING OUT
WOMEN, WAR, AND THE GLOBAL ECONOMY

Jan Haaken

Ariel Ladum

Seiza de Tarr

Kayt Zundel

Caleb Heymann

OOLIGAN PRESS
PORTLAND STATE UNIVERSITY

PUBLISHED BY OOLIGAN PRESS

Portland State University

P.O. Box 751 Portland, Oregon 97207-0751

Grateful acknowledgement is made for permission to include the following copyrighted material:

"Johnny Was"

Written by Bob Marley

©2005 Fifty Six Hope Road / Odnil Music Limited

Courtesy of The Bob Marley Foundation by arrangement with Fairwood Music USA

Used with permission in the accompanying DVD, Diamonds, Guns, and Rice: Sierra Leone and the Women's Peace Movement

All rights reserved.

"Just Say No!" and "How the IMF Helped Argentina" are courtesy of Barry Deutsch. Used with permission. All rights reserved.

Untitled Cartoon on 3:9 is courtesy of Tom Lechner. Used with permission. All rights reserved.

World Maps courtesy of the University of Texas.

Map of Africa courtesy of the Central Intelligence Agency.

Batik images created by artists from Freetown, Sierra Leone.

Cover photograph by Jessie Israel.

All other images by Jan Haaken, *et al.,* unless otherwise noted.

Jan Haaken, Ariel Ladum, Seiza de Tarr, Kayt Zundel, & Caleb Heymann

Speaking Out: Women, War, and the Global Economy

Published by Ooligan Press, Portland, Oregon

ISBN 1-932010-05-X CUSA

ISBN 978-1-932010-05-3

Printed in the United States of America

Section Four: Toward Peace and Reconciliation 4:1

Supplementary Resources 5:1

Sources 5:6

Introduction

Jan Haaken

Speaking Out: Women, War, and the Global Economy grew out of field research carried out over several years—research that included the production of a documentary video entitled *Diamonds, Guns, and Rice: Sierra Leone and the Women's Peace Movement*. As a teacher, researcher, and community activist, my work in recent decades has focused on violence, and particularly on the ways cultural contexts shape how stories of violence get told. While doing field research in 1999 in Guinea, I was drawn to the tens of thousands of Sierra Leoneans who had found refuge there as they escaped the civil war ravaging their country.

I became particularly interested in the stories of refugee women. One conversation stands out in my memory. A village woman informed me of a legend told throughout West Africa. "It is not good to send your children to America," she said, "for in America, they bury Africans in shallow graves." Through an interpreter, the woman explained her worry about youth mesmerized by the idea of America. The legend operated as a cautionary tale, it seemed, for youth captured by media images of the United States as a paradise of unlimited freedom.

Long after returning to the United States, this image of Africans buried in shallow graves haunted me. As a metaphor, the image spoke to me of American racism, and the cultural loss of memory in the U.S. concerning the legacy of slavery. In reviewing my videotaped interviews of women in refugee camps, I was caught between the desire to forget and the responsibility to remember. In a more dramatic and overwhelming way, the women interviewed were confronted with this same conflict. There was much to be learned from how these women approached the problem of how to forgive without forgetting—without covering over the problems that led to the war.

One important finding that emerged from these interviews was that the women had a broad range of stories to tell, both as victims and as adults who felt some responsibility for the problems that led to their civil war. The women held a variety of views on the causes of war and conditions for peace. I realized that their insights extended beyond their immediate crisis situation and that there was a great deal of value in bringing their stories to Westerners and particularly to students.

Building on Sierra Leonean women's accounts of the civil war, this curriculum introduces a series of questions concerning links between gender and war and provides tools for addressing those questions. Using the Sierra Leonean civil war as a case study, the curriculum guide, like the video documentary, brings into focus key forces operating behind the front lines of war zones—forces that continue to fuel armed conflict in regions throughout Africa, and other unstable areas of the world.

In showing *Diamonds, Guns, and Rice* to audiences at film festivals, universities, and high schools in the United States, many viewers wanted more information and tools for addressing the issues raised in the video. Many students were eager to get more involved. For example, one Portland State University student wrote to describe how she used the video in an introductory speech class: "Usually students in this kind of class doze off, but everyone was literally on the edge of their seats.... It was pretty awesome because it really reached people." This curriculum, *Speaking Out*, grew out of responses such as these, as well as discussions with teachers, community leaders, and peace activists. The book expands on themes introduced by the women featured in *Diamonds, Guns, and Rice*.

The curriculum and video are complementary components of this multi-media project, but each may be used independently. To introduce students to themes woven through *Speaking Out*, the documentary may be shown in its entirety prior to any of the classroom activities. The DVD format offers a menu for selecting parts of the documentary for specific lessons in different sections of the curriculum. Section Two: "Sierra Leonean Traditions" features the Introduction and Part I of the documentary ("Rice"), Section Three: "Globalism and the Economics of the Sierra Leonean Civil War" includes Part II ("Guns and Diamonds"), and Section Four: "Toward Peace and Reconciliation" presents Part III ("Peace"). The DVD format also includes four special features: "School Kids," "Rappers 4 Rights," "Sierra Leonean Truth and Reconciliation Commission: Voices of Women," and "The Diamond Trade: Discussion by Sierra Leonean-American Women." Just as the documentary tells a story that begins with the cultural context and moves through the decade of civil war and concludes with the peace process, so, too the curriculum follows this same progression of themes.

The Sierra Leonean Civil War: A Brief Overview

This curriculum educates students on the processes Sierra Leoneans underwent in constructing their own accounts of the civil war and the debates that arose over how to distribute responsibility for the widespread atrocities that occurred during the height of the conflict. There are many ways of telling the story of this civil war, and of explaining causal factors. *Speaking Out* provides tools for exploring these stories and for understanding some of the histories behind them. At the start, we set the stage for this journey into the war zone, beginning with locating Sierra Leone on a map. Sierra Leone is a small coastal country in West Africa, bordered by Guinea in the north and Liberia in the south. In telling the history of the civil war, *Speaking Out* explains the importance of this location, and how the histories of the United States and Sierra Leone are bound together through the brutal legacy of the slave trade. As a country rich in dramatic contrasts, from its cultural history to its physical terrain, Sierra Leoneans look back on a past filled with tales of epic proportions. There are, for example, bitter stories of the barbarism of the slave trade alongside inspiring accounts of the abolitionist campaign to establish Freetown as a colony for freed and escaped slaves.

The fighting that raged in Sierra Leone through the 1990s began in Liberia, a country also initially established as a colony for escaped slaves. *Speaking Out* investigates the history of this tense border, and how rebels loyal to Liberian leader Charles Taylor were able to cross the border to raid the diamond mines and recruit youth into their rebel movement. Some youths were abducted and others voluntarily joined the Revolutionary United Front (RUF), a rebel organization that degenerated from an opposition movement to a reckless band of rebels waging a campaign of terror across Sierra Leone in its bid for power. Understanding why this youth rebellion moved from legitimate grievances to terrorist acts, such as chopping off the limbs of villagers, emerged as one of the most puzzling and important questions taken up in the aftermath of the civil war.

The Sierra Leonean civil war, like many wars throughout history, did not conclude decisively with the formal signing of a peace treaty. By the time a peace treaty was brokered between the Sierra Leonean government and RUF commanders in 1999, much of Sierra Leone was in ruin. The war was declared officially over by the United Nations in 2002 after most of the combatants, including children as young as six years of age, were disarmed and demobilized. Key questions taken up in this curriculum concern how wars are brought to a close, and what conditions are important in establishing a framework for peace and reconciliation. This curriculum explores the minefield of issues that arise in the aftermath of civil war, and specifically the role of women in the peace process. In addition to the Truth and Reconciliation Commission (TRC) established in 1999 to determine the causes of the war, the Special Court of Sierra Leone was created several years later through the United Nations to prosecute senior commanders responsible for the most severe human rights abuses. Both of these mechanisms for reconciliation were recognized worldwide for including the accounts of women and youths and for addressing their grievances in the final recommendations.

The massive destruction, displacements, and trauma of war undermine the human capacity to move beyond immediate survival and for dialogue over the causes and consequences of war. Yet this curriculum builds on the idea—an idea that has taken hold in Sierra Leone in the aftermath of war—that people directly affected by war may learn from their traumatic experiences in ways that enable them to move on and to educate others on preventing armed conflict.

The Documentary Video

The documentary video *Diamonds, Guns, and Rice: Sierra Leone and the Women's Peace Movement* was produced by my son, Caleb Heymann, and me, in collaboration with Sierra Leonean peace activists in West Africa and the United States. We had the use of community access production facilities—one of the most important remaining public resources in the U.S. amidst the growing corporatization of media. Through the documentary we wanted to cast women not only as victims of war, but also as actively engaged in analyzing the causes of war and conditions for peace. We also wanted to place the violence of the war in a broader global context and to go beyond the crude portraits of barbaric rebels circulating in the mainstream American press. Enlisting a range of academic disciplines—history, economics, sociology, anthropology, literature, and my own field of psychology—we sought to go deeper into understanding the causes of war.

Diamonds, Guns, and Rice combines interviews, war footage, music, poetry, and photos portraying the vitality of the Sierra Leonean people and culture. Throughout the documentary, personal stories and photos are interwoven with analysis of the war and discussion of the peace process. Collecting photos for our documentary involved calls to Sierra Leoneans dispersed throughout the world. This process was both integral to the global activist nature of the project and a form of grieving for some participants. In war zones, whatever photos people possess are left behind as they flee to shelter. As we found photos to include in the documentary, we participated in memorializing the experiences of survivors. In addition to photographs, testimonials of refugee women capture the horror of the civil war and its devastating impact on women and children, as well as the active role they are taking in mobilizing for peace. Many of the women portrayed in the video also contributed to the curriculum guide.

Producing the video involved overcoming a series of obstacles in technology, geography, and culture. Much of the communication was through the spotty connections of cell phones. Even in 2005, years after the war was officially declared over, the electricity and land phones were often down for days, making communication difficult. Yet the women who contributed to the video and the curriculum persisted in *Speaking Out* in spite of these daunting obstacles, including the possibility of threats against their lives.

Educating about War

The classroom serves as an important site for addressing questions surrounding war and for developing critical tools to evaluate whether and when wars may be deemed just. Given that young people are the ones directly involved in military actions, educators have a particular responsibility to prepare youth to analyze the causes and consequences of war, as well as to consider conditions under which they might answer or resist a call to take up arms. In the wake of the attacks of September 11, passions ran high in the United States over the wisdom of military intervention. Open dialogue became one of the many casualties of the widening net of security operations at home and abroad. Teachers at my own university confessed to feeling uneasy about discussing the topic of war in the classroom. Nonetheless, schools remain vital spaces for promoting public dialogue on one of the more vexing moral questions in human history: Why war?

In producing *Diamonds, Guns, and Rice*, we were aware that creating a documentary around a war in Africa carried some difficult freight for teachers. Educators may find that it is complicated material that requires more time to explore than class schedules permit. For example, by focusing on distant wars and the corruption that fuels them, students may overlook the role their own government plays in armed conflict throughout the world. Similarly, students may view youth rebellions in Africa as part of a distant, ancient world of exotic rituals—without realizing that African youth are savvy consumers of hip-hop and rock, as well as movies and modern technology. Rebel fighters in the Sierra Leonean civil war took the names of characters from Western films, such as *Rambo*.

Gender, Youth, and War

In my own teaching in the area of gender and violence, I have found that students often bring to the courses a keen awareness of the association between masculinity and war but lack a deep understanding of how the two are related. Students know that war is commonly thought to be the business of adult men. From bloody combat on the battlefield to strategic maneuvering in the war room, socially organized violence tends to be cast as both a male right and responsibility. Yet the complexities of modern warfare defy such conventional wisdom, just as they challenge borders separating the battlefield and the home front. For example, casualties among noncombatants have steadily mounted over the last century. The United Nations Development Program concludes in their Human Development Report 1998 that civilian casualties rose from five percent in World War I to almost eighty percent in the late twentieth century.

This curriculum shows how war re-maps gender boundaries along with geographical boundaries. The activities explore how patriarchal societies are reproduced through warfare and how they also undergo various crises. Women often enter roles formerly carried out by men, or make new political demands as war widows or mothers of fallen soldiers. As women discover new strengths in taking on "men's jobs" on the home front, men discover vulnerabilities through the terrors of war. Throughout the world, women are entering fighting forces in larger numbers as well, just as they are demanding a greater say in the peace process.

Since youths played such a leading role in the Sierra Leonean civil war, including carrying out atrocities in their own villages, post-conflict interventions have focused heavily on the young. International relief efforts are still largely directed toward male combatants, however, rather than female youths affected by the war. *Speaking Out* focuses on the daunting barriers faced by girl combatants in the aftermath of the civil war. Some girls chose not to return to their communities because the war changed them in ways not readily reconciled with traditional female roles. Girls were victims of rape, abduction, and forced labor as cooks and armed soldiers, but they also defied conventional notions of girlhood and broke from traditional constraints. This small West African country provides an interesting context for global studies because its history includes many lessons in ethical conflicts as well, such as whether to accept former rebels back into their home communities that they previously attacked.

Sections of the Curriculum

Some of the content of *Speaking Out* is specific to the country of Sierra Leone, its history, and its peoples. But the curriculum includes ideas and activities that may be applied to a wide range of situations of armed conflict, holding vital lessons for those far removed from this war zone. The four sections of the curriculum are organized around key themes in the documentary video *Diamonds, Guns, and Rice*. Each section of the guide includes an introduction to the main theme of that part of the curriculum and lesson plans for classroom activities. The lesson plans were developed for a range of educational levels, from secondary schooling through college and adult education classes. High school and university students and teachers provided feedback on materials tested in the classroom and suggestions for developing options suitable to a range of academic abilities and backgrounds. Each section also features a story from a Sierra Leonean woman affected by the civil war as an entry point into the larger story of war, moving from the particular and local to the national and global forces that shaped their dramatic experiences. The guide concludes with a list of Supplementary Resources for further exploring topics introduced in *Speaking Out*.

Section One: Learning Across Cultural Boundaries establishes a portal of entry for studying Sierra Leone, particularly for teachers and students in the English-speaking world outside of Africa. In establishing an interdisciplinary framework for a case study of Sierra Leone, this section also introduces learners to key roles played by psychologists and researchers in war zones. This section presents lesson plans for looking at the cultural baggage learners may carry into cross-cultural inquiry. One activity includes an interview with Susan Shepler, a cross-cultural researcher examining dilemmas around reintegrating child soldiers. Another activity presents a story from Emma Fofanah, who is featured in *Diamonds, Guns, and Rice*. Fofanah, a Sierra Leonean woman living in the United States, tells of her struggle to cope with the devastating effects of the civil war on her family and homeland.

Section Two: Sierra Leonean Traditions takes learners into the "back roads" of Sierra Leonean society. Students learn about the role of women in carrying out work and cultural practices, and how the roles of women and men were affected by a decade of civil war. This section includes three lesson plans, one based on the story of Fatima Bona, a Sierra Leonean woman featured in the documentary, and the others organized around the role of women in rice farming and the social history of agricultural practices in Sierra Leone. Through this journey into the historical context, students and teachers gain insights into factors that produce resilience in the Sierra Leonean people.

Section Three: Globalism and the Economics of the Sierra Leonean Civil War carries learners behind the scenes of the Sierra Leonean civil war and introduces key players in the conflict. The struggle over resources figures prominently in the dynamics of the civil war. But the players who control banks, diamond interests, and the gun trade determine many of the rules of engagement. One lesson plan introduces Cecilia Bangura, a community leader featured in the documentary, as she discusses her perspective on global economic institutions. This section places armed conflict in a global context, focusing on how women are affected by battles over control of national resources.

Section Four: Toward Peace and Reconciliation shows how reparation and healing take many forms. This section introduces learners to the Special Court and the Truth and Reconciliation Commission, two key mechanisms adopted after the Sierra Leonean civil war to address the causes of the war and to make recommendations for the prevention of future armed conflict. This section of the curriculum emphasizes the role of women and youth in the peace process, from participation in cultural practices to political mobilization and economic development.

Section One: Learning Across Cultural Boundaries

Journeys begin with a series of preparations, from studying maps, to buying tickets, to packing suitcases. Less carefully scrutinized than passports and suitcases, however, are the cultural assumptions travelers carry to a foreign country—often termed cultural baggage. Cultural baggage refers to conscious and unconscious concepts of the world based on the particular social location or background of the individual. This may take the form of assuming a single standard of values or universal ideas of morality. For instance, a number of the American students we met in the course of traveling to West Africa were incensed with the system of bribery that operated throughout the region, comparing this system with "honest people back home." We were blocked at various junctures in the roads by small bands of youth who had put up a rope and wanted some change or cigarettes before lowering the barrier for our car to pass. Whether we describe this as an informal toll or highway robbery, the practice grew out of limited opportunities youth have to generate income.

A healthy dose of cultural relativism—evaluating actions, beliefs and practices relative to the specific cultural context in which they occur—is as important as immunizations when entering foreign countries. Too much relativism can produce cynical detachment from the problems of a society—or support pre-existing prejudices. For example, travelers may come to the conclusion that extreme poverty is "just the way it is" and stop short of probing for the deeper reasons behind wide economic disparities. Too little relativism means carrying an excess of certainty about one's own cultural values. Maintaining the right balance between too much and too little relativism can be vital for learning.

Cultural relativism need not imply that all societal values are equally valid. It is possible to be critical of the practices of a society while attempting to understand factors that sustain particular ways of life. Further, cultural traditions are often contradictory in their effects. Polygamy, for example, commonly practiced in some areas of Africa, may both restrict women and grant them particular freedoms. Although this form of marriage, where men take multiple wives, does express male power over women, it also creates female communities with some degree of autonomy from men.

Whether as students or travelers, people carry with them images of foreign lands shaped by popular culture, e.g., television, movies, and music. In making the documentary, *Diamonds, Guns, and Rice: Sierra Leone and the Women's Movement*, we sought alternatives to standard media images in the United States. Many news reports covering the Sierra Leonean civil war during the 1990s portrayed the rebels as inexplicably violent and primitive in their methods. The primary rebels in the Sierra Leonean conflict were described as young black men brandishing machetes and carrying out atrocities, often amputating the limbs of civilians. In many media accounts, responsibility for the terrible suffering fell entirely on the rebels—what one Sierra Leonean woman interviewed for the documentary termed "the bad boys on the ground." These reported atrocities added to preexisting racist images of African "savagery." Wars in the less technologically advanced societies of Africa are more often cast as "dirty" and primitive in their methods. Military actions carried out by the United States in Afghanistan and Iraq, in contrast, are portrayed by the U.S. media as "clean," with their surgical strikes and computer-generated targets.

This first section includes five lesson plans, establishing a portal of entry into the Sierra Leonean civil war. In preparing students to screen the documentary video *Diamonds, Guns, and Rice* later in the curriculum, Lesson 1, "Sierra Leone in Context," provides a brief history of Sierra Leone. Lesson 2, "Images of Africa," encourages students to reflect on their own perceptions of Africa and how these are influenced by images in the media and popular culture. Caleb Heymann, co-producer of *Diamonds, Guns, and Rice*, and a high school student at the time the documentary was made, tells how the videotaping changed his perceptions of gender. This experience also led him onto his current path in the field of documentarymaking. Lesson 3, "Gender and War," introduces students to gender dynamics associated with war and the reconciliation process. Lesson 4, "Conceptions of Youth," features an interview with educator Susan Shepler, who discusses issues in cross-cultural research, such as cultural assumptions concerning the responsibility of youth for their participation in the violence of war. Lesson 5, "A Story from Emma Fofanah," introduces Emma Fofanah, one of the Sierra Leonean women featured in *Diamonds, Guns, and Rice*. Fofanah provides yet another entrée into the story of the civil war—one told from the perspective of a Sierra Leonean-American woman struggling to cope with the trauma of armed conflict in her homeland.

Lesson 1   Sierra Leone in Context

Time: Approximately 30 minutes

Materials:

> A world map or globe
>
> Handout: "Setting the Stage for Civil War in Sierra Leone"

Procedure:

> Have students locate Sierra Leone on a world map, using either a globe or map in the classroom.
>
> Distribute "Setting the Stage for Civil War in Sierra Leone." Allow students time to read the handout.
>
> Facilitate a class discussion based on the following questions:
>
>> What factors does the essay introduce in establishing a context for the civil war in Sierra Leone? What are some of the difficulties in separating external (e.g., colonialism) and internal (e.g., indigenous practices) factors to explain the root causes of the civil war?
>>
>> How might the historical context shape relationships between Sierra Leoneans and "helpers" from Western countries?
>>
>> Sierra Leone has implemented a Truth and Reconciliation Commission and a Special Court to help the country recover from the civil war. What are some of the differences in these processes? How do you think each contributes to the peace process?

Lesson 2   Images of Africa

Time: Approximately 50 minutes

Materials:

Handout: "Have Camera, Will Travel: A Student Perspective on Africa"

Procedure:

Ask students to generate a list of words or phrases they associate with Africa and Africans and write them on the board.

Divide the class into small groups (3–4 students). Ask students to discuss potential sources of such images in their groups.

Distribute "Have Camera, Will Travel: A Student Perspective on Africa." Allow students time to read the essay.

Facilitate a class discussion based on the following questions:

How were the student documentary-maker's perceptions influenced by his experiences traveling in West Africa?

What are your perceptions about where we get many of our images of Africa? How do these compare to the perceptions of Caleb Heymann?

Homework: Write a one-page essay illustrating how the student documentary-maker's perceptions of a group of people changed after visiting where they lived.

Lesson 3   Gender and War

Time: Approximately 50 minutes

Materials:

> Handout: "Gender, War, and Community Reparation"

Procedure:

> Distribute "Gender, War, and Community Reparation." Allow students time to read the essay.

> Facilitate a class discussion based on the following questions:

>> What are two differences described by Haaken in how women and men experience war? What are two dilemmas women face in the reconciliation process?

>> According to Haaken, how does war break down traditional social structures? How might women benefit from these changes? How might these changes affect traditional roles of women and men?

>> Haaken describes how relief workers working with refugees may impose their own agenda rather than prioritizing issues of most concern to the women in the camps. Identify and discuss three principles that may guide relief workers in avoiding this pitfall.

Homework: Ask students to write a two-page essay summarizing potential differences in how women and men experience armed conflict and the reconciliation process.

Lesson 4   Conceptions of Youth

Time: Approximately 50 minutes

Materials:

Handout: "Field Research: Interview with Susan Shepler"

Procedure:

Distribute "Field Research: Interview with Susan Shepler." Allow students time to read the interview.

Divide the class into small discussion groups (3–4 students). Ask groups to discuss the following questions:

What are some differences between Western and Sierra Leonean conceptions of youth?

According to Shepler, what is problematic about drawing on a Western conceptualization of youth to evaluate the responsibility of child soldiers in the civil war?

How do pressures differ for male and female combatants to produce stories that would allow tdhem to return to their villages?

Why do adults seem fearful of former combatants?

Facilitate a class discussion based on group responses to the questions above.

Homework: Ask students to write a one-page essay discussing challenges Western psychologists may confront in understanding how Sierra Leoneans distribute responsibility for the civil war, particularly to child soldiers.

Lesson 5   A Story from Emma Fofanah

Time: Approximately 50 minutes

Materials:

Handout: "Emma Fofanah's Story"

Procedure:

Distribute "Emma Fofanah's Story." Allow students time to read the narrative.

Divide the class into small discussion groups (3–4 students). Ask groups to discuss the following questions:

Would you describe Emma Fofanah as a survivor of the Sierra Leonean civil war? In what ways are there different kinds of survivors?

How is Fofanah's story similar to those of many other immigrants to the United States? What does her story suggest about the ties and "cultural baggage" that immigrants bring to the United States?

Identify three coping mechanisms that Fofanah enlists in managing her distress over the civil war in her homeland.

Facilitate a class discussion based on group responses to the questions above.

Setting the Stage for Civil War in Sierra Leone

Ariel Ladum

Sierra Leone is a small coastal country in West Africa, bordered by Guinea in the north and east and Liberia in the south. In 1787 over three hundred "Black Poor" and about 100 whites left Britain to establish a British colony of Sierra Leone managed by the British Sierra Leone Company. Sierra Leone also has historical ties to the United States through the brutal legacy of the slave trade. America was a primary market for slave labor, and Sierra Leone was a prized region for slave traders bringing captives to build the plantation economy of the South. In 1792, 1,200 freed slaves seeking refuge from the American War of Independence joined the surviving settlers of the Colony—many of whom had died from harsh living conditions. This second influx established "Freetown" as the first permanent settlement. Sierra Leone did not become a Crown Colony of Britain until the 1808 downfall of the British Sierra Leone Company.

As the first modern political state in sub-Saharan Africa, Sierra Leone benefited from developments in infrastructure, although the indigenous peoples suffered under colonial domination. The British built railways and roads, as well as the first university in the region—Fourah Bay College. Improved intra-state transportation facilitated the exploitation of Sierra Leone's rich natural resources, particularly diamonds. Colonizers started recruiting men to work in migratory labor camps, and many young men left their communities to seek their fortunes in the diamond mines. Soon, however, the fantasy of getting rich through mining for diamonds proved illusory. Whether working for paltry wages in the mines or sifting through the mud for a few crude stones, young men often returned to their villages as poor as when they left.

During the period of African anti-colonial movements after World War II, black Sierra Leoneans resisted British rule, and gained independence in 1961. Immediately following this victory Sierra Leone's future looked bright—new roads were built and many hospitals, schools, and clinics opened. This hopefulness was short-lived, however. Sierra Leoneans struggled to survive under a series of corrupt leaders who continued to exploit the country's abundant diamond reserves for their own enrichment. By the mid 1980s, the country was mired in rapidly expanding foreign debt, rampant inflation, currency devaluation, budget deficits, and declining exports fueled in part by a growing informal economy largely based on an illicit diamond trade. Faced with frequent blackouts, food and fuel shortages, and unemployment, Sierra Leoneans had reached a state of desperate crisis.

Some have offered singular explanations—such as greed over diamonds or unbearable living conditions—for the rise of a rebel movement in March 1991. Factors underlying civil war in Sierra Leone are complex, however, linked to problems throughout West Africa—problems that, in turn, are tied to contemporary Western economic policies and the legacy of colonialism.

As the colonizer, Britain established an institutional framework for later economic exploitation of Sierra Leone. The British model of economic development in Sierra Leone consisted of exporting raw materials for manufacturing abroad; Sierra Leone itself had virtually no industry. In order to acquire raw materials colonial rulers manipulated the customary chieftaincy system—in which Paramount Chiefs acted as local government in provincial areas—transforming traditional leaders into agents of colonial power. Thus, rather than equipping Sierra Leone with a solid bureaucratic structure to provide strong governance, British colonialism left Sierra Leone with a de-centralized system of patronage in which citizens benefited more from alliances to local chiefs than from allegiance to the government in Freetown.

Post-independence regimes followed the example set by colonial powers. Successive governments continued to exploit traditional systems in order to sustain an export-based economy, granting cooperative Paramount Chiefs greater power, assets and wealth, overlooking particular smuggling operations, and awarding cabinet, civil service, and army appointments to certain ethnic groups. In turn, lower-level leaders granted favors such as land, mining licenses, and protection to their own supporters who provided political backing, manual labor, and social deference. Some supporters were financed entirely by local leaders, and naturally more loyal to them than to the more removed government.

Sierra Leonean state leaders were also involved in their own patronage system involving arms traders in East Europe, the global diamond industry, and Western economic organizations. Government officials sacrificed the collective good of Sierra Leoneans to personally benefit economically from these international players. Government officials would turn a blind eye to diamond smuggling or establish unequal trading relationships in exchange for arms. They set very low buying prices and export taxes for diamonds and cash crops that benefited global markets, and cut spending on social services to qualify for more loans from the World Bank and International Monetary Fund (IMF).

All of these factors have been identified as primary in creating conditions conducive to the outbreak of civil war. By subverting traditional systems of governance and mismanaging Sierra Leone's assets to serve private interests, political elites created a state of chronic deprivation and poverty for the general public. Divisions between a minority of rich political elites and very poor masses continued to grow. Few prospects for work, and limited health care, education, and other social services created deplorable living conditions.

The powerful elites used brutal tactics—including the death penalty—to silence any political opposition. The youths, abandoned by leaders who were unable to meet their basic needs, felt powerless to change their inhumane conditions and lost hope for a better future.

In the early 1990s the Liberian civil war spilled over into Sierra Leone and young men took up the fight to depose corrupt governments on both sides of the border. Fighters from the National Patriotic Front of Liberia (NPFL), led by Charles Taylor, joined with disenfranchised, radicalized students and disillusioned elements within the Sierra Leonean Army (SLA), as well as foreign mercenaries from the Ukraine and fighters from Burkina Faso, to form the rebel group, Revolutionary United Front (RUF). After Charles Taylor became President of Liberia in 1997, the Liberian government supplied the RUF with arms and training in exchange for looted goods and diamonds mined illegally by the rebels.

The Lomé Accord of July 1999 between the RUF and Sierra Leonean government eventually brought hostilities to an end, but not before years of fighting took a tremendous toll on the country. The groups involved in the fighting—the Revolutionary United Front (RUF), as well as the rebel organization of the Armed Forces Revolutionary Council (AFRC), the Sierra Leonean Army (SLA), and the Civil Defense Forces (CDF)—waged war not only against each other, but also against civilians. During the civil war an estimated 12,000 children were separated from their families and forced into servitude. Although estimates vary, of the 4.2 million citizens of Sierra Leone at least 75,000 were killed, over one million were displaced within the country, more than 500,000 became refugees, and in excess of 400,000 people had at least one limb amputated.[1] Although all fighting factions employed brutal tactics against the civilian population—including murder, mutilation, amputation, slavery, rape, and kidnapping—the RUF was found responsible for the largest number of human rights abuses.[2] In fact many critics insist that the Lomé Peace Accord was a terrible denouement to the bloody conflict because it rewarded the RUF; rather than punishing the military commanders, the negotiators granted immunity from prosecution as well as four ministry positions in exchange for demobilization of the rebel forces.

The Lomé Accord called for the creation of a Truth and Reconciliation Commission (TRC). Purposes of the TRC included rebuilding relationships, preventing future conflict, and creating a balanced historical account of violations and abuses of human rights and international humanitarian law. Although formally established by the Sierra Leone Parliament in February 2000 by virtue of the Truth and Reconciliation Act, the TRC did not start hearing testimony until April 2003, issuing a final report in October 2004. In addition to the Truth and Reconciliation Commission, in January 2002 the United Nations and the government of Sierra Leone jointly created the Special Court for Sierra Leone to punish the worst human rights offenders and bring restitution to victims. The vast majority of people indicted by the Special Court are Sierra Leonean. Many Sierra Leoneans, however, lay considerable responsibility for the conflict at the feet of Charles Taylor, the former Liberian President. On March 7, 2003, the prosecutor approved indictments against Charles Taylor and former AFRC leader Johnny Paul Koroma. Charles Taylor fled his country and sought refuge in Nigeria, where, as of 2005, he remains, fighting extradition. The CDF trial began on June 3, 2004, the RUF trial began on July 5, 2004, and the three AFRC accused were brought to trial in March 2005. As of July 2005, three leaders of the former CDF, three leaders of the former RUF, and three leaders of the former AFRC were indicted for multiple counts of war crimes, crimes against humanity, and other serious violations of international humanitarian law.

Sources:

Akrinade, B. (2001). International Humanitarian Law and the Conflict in Sierra Leone. *Notre Dame Journal of Law, Ethics and Public Policy, 15*, 391–454.

Keene, D. (2003). Greedy Elites, Dwindling Resources, Alienated Youths: The Anatomy of Protracted Violence in Sierra Leone. *International Politics and Society, 2.* Retrieved from http://fesportal.fes.de/pls/portal30/docs/FOLDER/IPG/IPG2_2003/ARTKEEN.HTM

Pratt, D. (1999). *Sierra Leone: The Forgotten Crisis.* Retrieved from http://www.sierra-leone.org/pratt042399.html

Schocken, C. (2002). *The Special Court for Sierra Leone: Overview and Recommendations.* Retrieved from http://www.law.berkeley.edu/faculty/ddcaron/Public_Website/Courses/Intl%20cts/Semina-%20Fall%202001/2001-Schocken-on-Sierra-Leone.htm

Sierra Leone Truth and Reconciliation Commission. (2004, October). *Sierra Leone Truth and Reconciliation Commission.* Overview, Chapter 2, and Chapter 3 retrieved July 2005, from United States Institute of Peace Web site: http://www.usip.org/library/tc/tc_regions/tc_sl.html#rep

The Special Court for Sierra Leone. *The Special Court for Sierra Leone: Basic Facts.* Retrieved from http://www.sc-sl.org/index.html

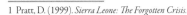

1 Pratt, D. (1999). *Sierra Leone: The Forgotten Crisis.* Retrieved from http://www.sierra-leone.org/pratt042399.html

2 Sierra Leone Truth and Reconciliation Commission. (2004, October). *Sierra Leone Truth and Reconciliation Commission.* Overview, Chapter 2, and Chapter 3 retrieved July 2005, from United States Institute of Peace Web site: http://www.usip.org/library/tc/tc_regions/tc_sl.html#rep

Have Camera, Will Travel: A Student Perspective on Africa

Caleb Heymann

In 2004 Caleb Heymann graduated from Pomona College with a B.A. in History. He is currently studying at AFDA film school in Cape Town, South Africa.

In the summer of 1999, between my junior and senior years of high school, I had the opportunity to travel to West Africa with my mother, Jan Haaken, to visit my cousin, a Peace Corps volunteer in Guinea. Having previously learned the basics of video production through Flying Focus Video Collective, a Portland-based group of activist videographers, I decided to take a camera along. I was not prepared, however, for what lay ahead. What began as a family vacation developed into a life-changing experience.

The first stop was Senegal, the country neighboring Guinea. I landed in Dakar, Senegal's bustling capital, with two suitcases—one stuffed with lightweight clothes, the other containing a Hi-8 video camera, a couple dozen blank tapes, and a barely functional tripod built for still photography. I also arrived with an unrealistic expectation of what it would take to translate raw footage into a documentary. If someone had told me about the mind-numbing tedium of logging hours of footage, searching for photos and additional video material, or editing in an outdated analog studio, I may very well have turned around and caught the first flight back home. Instead, I came into the trip open-minded and curious.

Despite knowing little about video film, I did know a few things coming into the project. I realized that there was—and is—a tradition of Westerners documenting African cultures in a way that oversimplifies or otherwise misunderstands their reality. For centuries, African cultures have been understood as "primitive" in opposition to "civilized" Western cultures. The concept of primitive cultures often includes racist stereotypes of Africa as a continent of brutal savages. In my African History course, for example, I learned about Western biases in how resistance movements were typically portrayed. When black Africans rebelled against the colonial powers in the 1960s, Western media often focused more on threats to white colonizers than on the suffering of black Africans. More liberal accounts viewed black Africans as helpless victims of bloody conflicts. While the victim model may have been a step up from the savage model, it nonetheless continued to strip Africans of their identities as complex individuals.

It was important for me to understand some of this history before picking up the camera. While it is easy to think of the camera as an objective recorder of physical reality, a cameraperson makes many decisions that influence how the subject is portrayed; one must decide both what to shoot and how to shoot it. Technical aspects—including camera angle, lighting, depth of field, and zoom—all contribute to messages communicated to the viewer. For the visual focus I felt it was important to film the subjects in a way that emphasized their individuality while also capturing the horrifying circumstances in which they lived in the aftermath of war. Although I could not become a cultural insider, I wanted to convey the African perspective on the conflict as much as possible and avoid letting my personal values dominate the choices I made with the camera.

Although you never shed your own cultural baggage, there are ways a filmmaker can interact respectfully in a foreign country. For me, this meant listening before speaking. It meant being willing to learn from people of other cultures. For example, I found that saying "hello" takes a long time in Africa, and that you first must ask questions like, "how is your mother, how is your father, your sister," before getting to the point of your visit. These long greetings were reminders that we are always part of a larger group rather than simply standing as an individual. This custom also reminded me that what one culture considers an efficient use of time may be considered rude in another. Historically, Westerners have imposed their values onto African cultures in the process of colonization. By listening and learning first, however, one can begin to counterbalance the injustices of history and respect other cultures. I learned that filmmaking of this type requires respectful collaboration with the community being filmed. We talked to people about the issues we were exploring in the documentary, and tried to get their ideas about what images to include. In refugee camps, we discussed how women wanted to present some of the reasons for the war.

What I learned through the process of gathering footage made me think more about gender. I had grown up in a community of political activists for whom sexual equality was a central issue, and this trip opened my eyes to the range of struggles facing women in Sierra Leone. Sometimes the sexism operated in subtle ways, such as a husband "offering" to sit in the room during the interview when his wife spoke about the concerns of women in her village. Women also seemed to do most of the physical labor as men sat and socialized. Throughout my trip I often saw women out in the fields farming with hand tools, or carrying large buckets of water and heavy loads of produce on their heads on their way home or to market. At the same time, many of the interviews and informal discussions my mother and I had with women revealed how traditions such as polygamy that seemed blatantly unjust to me were in fact more complex than they initially seemed. Some women insisted that having

other wives to help take care of their husband actually liberated them from many domestic responsibilities and gave them a sense of independence from their husbands. Older women, in particular, held considerable authority in the villages despite not having the property rights or legal rights of men.

This documentary would not have been possible without footage from Sierra Leoneans who often risked their lives to document the war. Much of the material we gathered for the documentary was recorded on second-rate equipment and duplicated several times, with picture quality deteriorating with each copy. Grassroots activists sent copies of a video to a friend in one country and then on to someone in the next. The scene of young soldiers marching through the streets of Freetown, for example, was originally filmed by DDwin Kamara from behind a curtain in a hotel room. Even though the tape was in its third generation by the time we procured a copy, we felt that including this grainy footage was important in offering a first-hand account of the war. Although American students are accustomed to high production values in films and electronic media, particularly work that comes out of Hollywood, the unpolished quality of the images in *Diamonds, Guns, and Rice: Sierra Leone and the Women's Peace Movement* creates its own aesthetic—one more common to international teams working with videographers and activists in third world countries.

When we returned home to the States to produce the documentary, we realized the importance of communicating a sense of hope rather than despair over this war zone in West Africa. Much of the material we received from

Sierra Leoneans and news outlets depicted gruesome acts of violence. It would have been easy to create a documentary that simply documented the horror of the civil war through accounts of the victims of maiming, rape, and other dreadful crimes. Yet *Diamonds, Guns, and Rice* goes beyond the victimization of Sierra Leoneans by focusing on the progressive struggle of determined women to bring peace and justice to their country. The documentary deals with individuals who were able to survive and remain hopeful through horrific circumstances. I believe the documentary is a small step toward recognizing the richness and resilience of African cultures.

As a student, my experience with this project brought into focus my own goals and reminded me why it was important to go beyond the borders of my homeland. Life is extremely difficult in West Africa, yet people also have a great capacity to enjoy life. There is less reliance on the hundreds of products we require to get through the day—from countless cleaning products to an array of electronic gadgets—and much more emphasis on being resourceful and using what you have. In returning to the United States, I felt more part of an international community and developed a passion for progressive uses of media. The pictures of Africa in mainstream media such as television shows, commercials, and movies, do not tell the real story. Alternative media can tell stories that would not be told on the major networks. Media centers, cable access networks, and video collectives offer valuable opportunities for young people to work in film, radio, and television at little or no cost. My hope is that *Diamonds, Guns, and Rice* will inspire other students to experiment with these facilities and venture into the unknown.

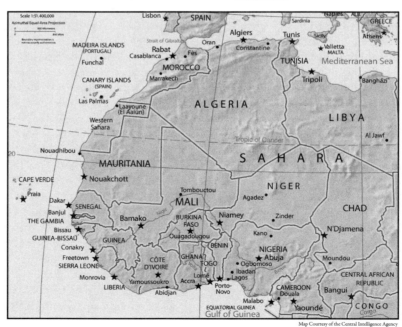

Map Courtesy of the Central Intelligence Agency

Gender, War, and Community Reparation

Jan Haaken

While I was carrying out research in West Africa in 1999, I visited a village in Guinea where my niece, Jessie, was working as a Peace Corps volunteer. On the day of our arrival, a group of women came out to welcome us. An elderly woman, her stooped shoulders wrapped in an elegant pink shawl, placed her hand on my breast. Initially startled, I soon realized that the gesture was intended to be friendly. As the elderly one continued to gently pat my chest, Jessie translated the conversation that ensued. She explained that the breast—as a source of nurture—was symbolically linked to a female line of authority. Jessie told the women who had gathered that although she had not "sucked from my breast" as an infant, her aunt and her mother had both "sucked from the same breast." After Jessie established my place within a matrilineal kinship system, the women concluded that I was to be received as a mother of Jessie—as part of what African and African-American communities term "other mothers."

For me, being welcomed into a fold of strangers was a moving experience—a reminder of the human capacity for connectedness and openness to outsiders. After participating in a number of global conferences on women, this experience in West Africa deepened my sense of international sisterhood. Broader and more egalitarian than motherhood, the kinship of sisters served as a guiding metaphor for my research focused on women's experiences with war. Yet I try to be conscious of the danger that this concept of sisterly affiliation may create a false sense of similarity and overlook ways I and others (women *and* men) carry the legacy of colonialism into our interactions across cultural borders.

Gender and War

My previous research as a clinical and cultural psychologist focused on trauma, collective remembering, and storytelling.[1] I have been particularly interested in how women draw on different cultural resources than men in narrating disturbing life experiences. Females are granted more latitude in expressing vulnerable feelings, such as fear and dependency, whereas males are given more freedom to express active emotions, such as anger, aggression, and dominance. The social boundaries established between masculine and feminine worlds of experience shape defenses involved in remembering as well. Male war stories often include idealized images centered on heroic action and stoical endurance. From World War I through the Vietnam War and war in Iraq, however, veterans groups have challenged the dominant discourse of masculinity, emphasizing the emotional and physical costs of repressing feelings more often associated with the "feminine"—for example, vulnerability, terror, and dependency. The movement in the aftermath of the Vietnam War to address post-traumatic stress disorder among veterans groups grew out of this broader critique of a stoical and militaristic ideology of manhood.

Throughout the world, women are less apt to glorify war than are men—in part because the roles they play in warfare, whether as victims or war effort supporters, are less exalted. Men are more apt than women to die in bloody conflicts, and soldiering holds a more central place in masculine identity. Male soldiers are seen as heroes, but after the smoke clears from the battlefield, women are left to care for the wounded and mourn for the dead. Women also suffer the stigma of rape (a common crime of war) and are shunned due to pregnancies and babies born of war. Yet even though women bear more of the hidden trauma of war, this does not imply that women are by nature peacemakers. From revolutionary struggle to military crusades, for just and unjust causes, women throughout history have succumbed to "war fever" and have joined men in defense of their country, clan, or class.

Gender also structures societal patterns of remembering. Whereas the war stories of men are often romanticized, women's accounts—set on the home front or the battlefield—are more apt to be forgotten altogether in the official chronicles of war. Even as researchers, journalists, and feminists increasingly address women's accounts of war,[2] older gender scripts continue to shape the structure of female narratives. One of these older scripts of female victimization portrays a beguilingly helpless woman fending off a rapacious villain (often a dark-skinned man). In this stereotypical plot, the good guy enters the scene to save the damsel in distress from the bad guy. In the course of carrying out research for the documentary documentary *Diamonds, Guns, and Rice* and this curriculum, I found that media reports of the Sierra Leonean civil war often drew on this formulaic story. The Western powers were cast as the righteous warriors called upon to save the good Africans (the women and children) from the bad Africans

1 See Haaken, J. (1998). *Pillar of Salt: Gender, Memory and the Perils of Looking Back*. New Brunswick: Rutgers University Press; Haaken, J. (2002, Autumn). Cultural Amnesia: Memory, Trauma and War. *Signs: Journal of Women in Culture and Society, 28* (1), pp. 455–457; Haaken, J. (2002). The Good, the Bad, and the Ugly: Psychoanalytic and Cultural Perspectives on Forgiveness. In S. Lamb and J.G. Murphy (Eds.). *Before Forgiving: Cautionary Views of Forgiveness in Psychotherapy*. New York: Oxford University Press, pp. 172–191; Haaken, J. (2002). Stories of Survival: Class, Race, and Domestic Violence. In Nancy Holmstrom (Ed.). *The Socialist Feminist Project: A Contemporary Reader in Theory and Politics*. New York: Monthly Review Press, pp. 102–120; Haaken, J. (2003). Traumatic Revisions: Remembering Abuse and the Politics of Forgiveness. In P. Reavey and S. Warner (Eds.). *New Feminist Stories of Child Sex Abuse*. New York: Routledge, pp. 77–93.

2 For analyses of global politics, gender, and militarism, see, Christie, D. J., Wagner, R. V., & Winter, D. D. (2001). *Peace, Conflict, and Violence: Peace Psychology for the 21st Century*. Upper Saddle River, NJ: Prentice Hall; Enloe, C. (2000). *Bananas, Beaches and Bases: Making Feminist Sense of International Politics*. Berkeley: University of Berkeley Press; Giles, W. & Hyndman, J. (2004). *Sites of Violence: Gender and Conflict Zones*. Berkeley: University of Berkeley Press; Farr, K. (2004). *Sex Trafficking: The Global Marketing of Women and Children*. New York: Worth Publishers.

(the young rebels and the old chiefs). Left out of this story are the many ways that Western governments and commercial interests fuel the very conflicts in which they later intervene militarily. Also "repressed" in the scripting of these stories are the deeper grievances that lead some girls and women to join the rebel cause. Girls generated more sympathy when cast as violently abducted into the fighting forces rather than as voluntarily joining to escape forced marriages or compensate for a lack of economic opportunity.

In beginning a documentary documentary about the Sierra Leonean civil war, I struggled with the question of how to portray women who had undergone experiences quite different from my own. My work in the global feminist movement had deepened my appreciation for the profound difficulties women face in unstable societies such as Sierra Leone. At the same time, women throughout the world share many of the same burdens common to caregivers. Dialogue over a number of years with Sierra Leonean women—and some men—allowed me to work between the poles of commonality and difference, and to construct a more nuanced picture of the relationship between gender and war.

Part of that complex picture is placing male violence in the context of colonial exploitation and the ravaging effects of the global economy. Since colonial times, men have left their villages to find work in labor camps, working under dehumanizing conditions for paltry wages. Attachments between men and women—and between men and their communities—have been shaped by this complicated and traumatic history. While it is important to confront traditional practices that foster violence against women, it is also important to emphasize *structural violence* as both a cause and a consequence of war. Structural violence refers to harm that communities suffer as the result of institutional policies, such as those imposed by the International Monetary Fund (IMF) and the World Bank as conditions for development loans. Structural Adjustment Programs, for example, imposed by the IMF shortly before the Sierra Leonean civil war broke out, required the government to cut back on public sector services, such as health care, education, and food subsidies in order to finance the loans. Women, youth, and the poor are particularly vulnerable to these policies that reduce social welfare spending by the state. When there are shortages of necessary resources, whether land, food, and water, or education and health care, those with less social status often go without. Under these conditions, women, in their roles as caregivers and local producers, are forced to work even harder to make ends meet.

Patriarchy, Feminism, and the Anti-Violence Movement

Patriarchy refers to legal, economic, and cultural practices organized around the power of senior males. Although the legal foundations of patriarchy were largely dismantled in Western countries by the late twentieth century, patriarchal practices continue to be reproduced in subtle—and not

so subtle—ways. Men still dominate senior positions in government, business, and the professions, even though women have successfully fought many forms of sexual discrimination. Many African countries remain patriarchal through customary laws granting men authority over wives and daughters, and progress is slowly being made to transform forms of authority oppressive to women.

Throughout history women have worked to improve their own lives and their communities. Over the last several hundred years, and particularly in the late twentieth century, women have come together to advance their interests collectively as part of a feminist movement. Yet many activists working on "women's issues"—such as reproductive health, childcare, or education for girls—are uncomfortable with the term *feminism,* either because they associate the term with Western culture or may understand their political interests as based on race, ethnicity, or class rather than on gender. Others identify as feminists but bring their own definitions and meanings to the term. For example, Sierra Leonean activist Yatta Samah, included in Sections One and Four of this curriculum, describes herself as an ecofeminist—a convergence of political feminism, environmentalism, and women's spirituality.

Beginning with the International Conference on Women held in Mexico City in 1975, organized through the United Nations, feminists worldwide have addressed the problem of gender violence as a human rights issue. Transnational women's movements of the 1990s and 2000s have organized to address gender violence and advance the universal rights of women. Many women are increasingly crossing national borders and entering conflict zones, often under the auspices of relief organizations, to initiate campaigns focused on the effects of war on women, from rape and prostitution, to poverty and homelessness.

Following the years of violence and the resulting displacements of hundreds of thousands of refugees fleeing the upheaval in Sierra Leone, nongovernmental organizations (NGOs) provided relief assistance for displaced victims. As in other conflict zones, international charitable organizations offered vital resources, such as shelter, food, and clean water, for Sierra Leonean refugees, both in the camps and in the resettlement of communities. When I arrived in 1999 along the border of Sierra Leone, I met a number of women from Western countries working tirelessly to provide assistance to the swelling numbers of war refugees. Though these relief workers no doubt had the best intentions, some Western feminists working through relief agencies may inadvertently impose their own agendas onto women in conflict zones. As an example, before bussing out to the refugee camps in Guinea I met with several rescue workers who were assisting women refugees in identifying victims of sexual violence. They told me that in the Massakoundou refugee camps women leaders were required to identify women and children who were victims of rape and prostitution in order to receive aid for a community garden. The aim of this requirement was to force refugee communities to confront the stigma of rape as well as other forms of sexual violence.

As important as addressing gender violence was, I wondered about the targeting of sexual violence in this assistance program, and whether this category of trauma may have been more salient for Western women than for the refugees. When I spoke with women in the camps about their concerns, they did speak of girls being sexually violated and women exchanging sex for food with men who raided relief trucks. But sheer exhaustion from securing food and taking care of children, primary responsibilities of women, emerged as a more chronic concern. While male sexual violence was a real issue, male passivity and abandonment of women were less apt to register as sources of female suffering to the Western aid workers.

Reconciliation, Forgiveness, and Collective Remembering

Women face specific challenges in the peace and reconciliation process. Throughout history women have operated as shock absorbers in conflict zones, serving as informal mediators, grief counselors, and caring for the sick and wounded. Following the civil war in Sierra Leone—a conflict that had engulfed the country and divided villages and even families—the problem of reintegrating ex-combatants into their communities concerned all Sierra Leonean citizens. But women shouldered a particularly heavy load in rehabilitating youths, many of whom were both victims and perpetrators.

Western counselors in post-conflict situations often emphasize the importance of victims talking about their experiences and of requiring perpetrators to listen to these testimonials. Belief in the therapeutic value of talk—of putting difficult experiences into words—is often associated with Western beliefs about emotional healing. Although many refugees and peace activists with whom I spoke emphasized talking about what had happened, they also stressed other activities as vital to healing, from dancing and singing, to traditional purification rituals, such as offering libations of water to the earth.

In public forums, interviews, and informal gatherings, Sierra Leonean women reflected on the varied meanings of the mandate to "forgive and forget," and whether forgiving required some capacity to forget. Some women insisted that, "we must put the war at our backs." Others used the metaphor of "turning the page of the book" in emphasizing the task of moving forward. Still other women cautioned that "we must not bury the past, or it will come up again and again." While seemingly contradictory, these responses reflected a vital dynamic in any post-war situation. The capacity to forget, to place experiences in the past, is as important as the capacity to remember. Too much forgetting makes it difficult to learn from traumatic experiences and to acknowledge their effects. But too much remembering keeps conflicts alive—and is associated with cycles of revenge.

Truth and Reconciliation Commissions (TRCs) serve as an important vehicle for collectively sharing responsibility for both the causes of war and the reparation process. In Sierra Leone, a TRC was mandated in the Lomé Peace Accord of 1999 and carried out in 2002–2003, during the same period that a Special Court for prosecuting war crimes was conducted. Hundreds of victims presented their stories in public forums before the TRC. Hundreds of perpetrators also told their stories, seeking the forgiveness of their communities. This group context for telling stories was vital to the process of reconciliation. An individual victim could refuse reconciliation with a particular perpetrator, but both parties could still participate in community reconciliation rituals.

For Westerners living beyond the conflict-zone, there is a moral mandate to support Sierra Leoneans as they gather up fragments of their war-torn past and rebuild their society. As Sierra Leoneans make reparations with one another, it remains up to the Western world—those who benefited from the legacies of slavery and colonialism—to make reparations with Africa. Some of this work is being carried out by governmental and nongovernmental organizations engaged in relief work, cultural and educational projects, and economic initiatives. But the work of reparation goes beyond addressing the immediate crisis of war and extends into the larger responsibilities we share as global citizens to build a more just and equitable world.

Field Research: Interview with Susan Shepler

Susan Shepler received her Ph.D. in Social and Cultural Studies in Education, University of California Berkeley. Her dissertation was on the reintegration of child soldiers and the perceptions of youth in Sierra Leone, and she has published in the areas of youth culture and post-conflict studies. Shepler was a Peace Corps volunteer in Sierra Leone during the 1980s. Beginning in the late 1990s, she spent 18 months carrying out research with child soldiers in their home communities.

Haaken: One focus of *Diamonds, Guns, and Rice: Sierra Leone and the Women's Peace Movement* is the effect of the Sierra Leonean civil war on youth. In expanding on that issue here, let's start with what we mean by youth. How is the boundary drawn in Sierra Leone between childhood and adulthood?

Shepler: It's difficult to speak of a strictly Sierra Leonean conception of youth. Concepts of youth have been very much shaped by contact with Western countries, especially England, over several centuries. For example, formal public education in Sierra Leone has operated under the British since the 1780s, with missionaries providing much of the funding.

Haaken: How has this history influenced understanding of childhood as well as the actual experiences of youth?

Shepler: The actual experiences of youth match many of the stereotypes Westerners have of children in the developing world: that they are devalued, work long hours, and that relationships within the family are different in some respects than in the U.S. Children are exchanged across kinship groups in a way that cements family bonds that have an economic basis. For instance, a village family may marry one of their young daughters to a much older cousin working abroad as a means of bringing income to the entire family.

One thing that NGOs (nongovernmental organizations) have been interested in when developing programs for the reintegration of former child combatants is the existing tradition of child fosterage. Children could be sent to an aunt, or sent to someone for apprenticeship, or for religious education. Building on this tradition may make it easier for children in post-war Sierra Leone to find caring families with whom to live.

Haaken: How are youth initiated into adulthood?

Shepler: In earlier times, youth would be "in the bush" with adults for months to learn traditional skills specific to their sex. Adults would be in charge of training youth for several years before they were fully initiated. Even with the increased mobility of people, including youth, there are still ties to specific locales, and that is now one of the main functions of traditional initiation practices—to tie children to the location of their parents and

their tribe. Even before the war, the initiation process had undergone tremendous change over earlier times. As more and more children attended formal Western style schools, there was less time for them to be sequestered for initiation training. Now training in the bush is usually a matter of days rather than months. Students will come home from school for their initiation, which may be done during holidays. In urban places, initiation practices have particularly eroded and the mix of ethnic groups has led to a crisis over what constitutes authentic traditional practices. The war has further shattered these traditions.

The traditional practices still play an important role in formally marking the boundary between youth and adulthood, in that one cannot be said to be an adult unless one has been initiated. However, initiation alone does not make one an adult. I believe that being a student has become a more important marker of "youth" in many respects. The initiation as a marker between stages of life has weakened, even though it is still an important part of the culture.

Haaken: Earlier, you said that Sierra Leoneans have had contact with Western ideas for centuries, including ideas about youth. In the United States, particularly, youth is associated with a state of pure innocence. How are these Western ideas about youth being played out now—in the aftermath of the war?

Shepler: The issue of child soldiering moves many people in the West since what happens to children is thought to be the most important. There is less concern about what happens to adults.

This Western view that children are innocent and morally pure in a way totally separate from adults seems weird to Sierra Leoneans. That doesn't mean that they don't value children.

Now this notion of the innocence of the child is being taken up by children and communities, but in a new way. "It's not my fault because I am a child..."

Haaken: The issue of the rights of the child is an important one, though, and has become one of the more progressive worldwide movements of the last century, along with the rights of women. How would you separate what is progressive about this movement from what is not so progressive—specifically in relation to Sierra Leone?

Shepler: Our notion of the rights of the child in the United States involves a cutoff, whereby before the age of 18 you don't know what you are doing, and after that you do. Traditionally, Sierra Leoneans have had a more complex view of childhood; an uninitiated child would not be held responsible in the sense of being expected to make reparation for violations against the community, but an initiated child would not be inevitably responsible either. They do have a conception of individual responsibility, but violations of societal rules—whether by children or adults—are thought to be the family's responsibility as well.

Haaken: How are the rights of the Sierra Leonean child being addressed relative to the issue of child soldiers?

Shepler: In the process of bringing youths back into society, there is an emphasis on stories that relieve youths of responsibility for the war. The Western notion of youth as innocence gets extended into the idea that, "it's not my fault because I was abducted or drugged." This story allows the return of youths to their communities, partly because western NGOs influence the conditions of their return.

Haaken: But many youths were drugged or abducted into the Revolutionary United Front (RUF). Are you saying they should be held responsible for the violence they participated in?

Shepler: The issue of responsibility is a complicated one. Youths are not ultimately responsible, but many of these young people also chose to join the rebels. That choice was based on very desperate situations, however. What gets lost is children's agency—their power to act on the world around them—and the legitimacy of many of their grievances. And it reinforces patriarchy, the authority of the elders. What I find problematic is the idea that someone under 18 and someone over 18 are understood so differently. These numbers have little meaning in the Sierra Leone context. But because they are used by the United Nations and other NGOs, they are affecting the definition of youth in Sierra Leone.

Haaken: How is this different for boys than for girls?

Shepler: In terms of gender, girls have suffered most because they have broken the rules of adulthood and girlhood. Girls who were rebels also have been able to shake up the rules. Now, a lot of girl mothers have been able to go to school, because they can lay claim to this notion that the war ruined them sexually, but that it is not their fault. What is interesting to me is the extent to which girls are less able to use the Western notion of child innocence that is so effectively used by boys. That means they need to find a different path to reintegration.

Haaken: The notion that all girls were abducted leaves out the troubling question of whether some were voluntarily involved to varying degrees in a rebellion, which, as terrible as the violence was, may have been legitimate. There are many possible stories of why youths participated in the war, but the innocent child story is the only one that is granted real legitimacy.

Shepler: Yes, and it plays out differently for girls than for boys. Boys can be put back into the system more easily than girls. Girls aren't as readily integrated into the old system since the war. People will often say that the war has spoiled the girls, that many have become prostitutes. Although this is partly true, and is an effect of war and poverty throughout the world, this notion that the girls have all become prostitutes also covers over a much more complex reality for girls. Many girls who were with the rebels now don't want to go back to their villages. They are pushing for new skills.

So many things are changing, particularly for girls. This war was a crisis of youth; still the crisis opens up possibilities for transforming the society in positive, progressive ways.

Haaken: Could you give an example of that?

Shepler: When there was a school closed for lack of payment of teachers' salaries while I was in Freetown in 2001, students went out on strike. They marched down the street in protest. So this was a very positive form of youth mobilization without taking up arms. Although the youths were protesting in a non-violent way, many adults cast them as rebels, which is akin to portraying them as terrorists. So there is this tremendous fear of youths as a result of the war, as well as youths overcoming their own fear of elders. School walkouts are not new, but adults' fear of groups of youths in the streets is.

Haaken: Do youths have a greater political voice in the aftermath of the war?

Shepler: Actually, I don't know if I would say that youth's have new power in Sierra Leone. They have new access to Western ideas about youth which are rights-based, more global, and funded by NGOs. But these ideas don't extend very far into the country-side, and my argument is that in accepting this Western model of youth, they are giving up an indigenous form of youth power that come from initiation and adult status achieved through rites of passage.

The story is different for girls for two reasons. First, they had so little power under the indigenous system that the Western system is a big improvement. Second, ironically, they are less able to use the innocence argument because their sexual activity—forced or not—exempts them from being innocent youth. Essentially, girls are either pretending that nothing happened to them in order to reintegrate into their villages, or they are going to the cities to fend for themselves. Neither of these is a great outcome, but the point is that they are making less use of Western assumptions about youth in formulating their post-war social strategies.

Emma Fofanah's Story

Emma Fofanah grew up in a large family in the town of Makeni in the northern part of Sierra Leone, situated on the West Coast of Africa. Emma's father had two wives and she grew up surrounded by many brothers and sisters. Her mother had ten children and her father's other wife had five children. Growing up they all lived together on a big compound. Each wife had her own house and garden, and grew all the vegetables used for cooking. When Emma was a child it was not common for girls to be educated, especially if there were male children. In her family, however, education was a priority. Her father decided that despite having very little money, he would provide an education for each of his children. Although the family was Muslim, Emma's father sent her and her sisters to the Catholic school, the only school available for girls. After finishing high school in Makeni, Emma attended technical college. In 1987, Emma immigrated to Portland, Oregon with her two children joining her husband there. After completing a degree at the Western Business College, Emma took a position as a sterile-processing technician at Oregon Health Sciences University. Since coming to the United States, Emma has returned to Sierra Leone once, in 1992, to visit her mother after Emma's father passed away. The civil war that engulfed Sierra Leone in the 1990s took a terrible toll on Emma and her family. The town of Makeni Emma remembers was a very beautiful and safe place to live. But during the civil war rebels from the Revolutionary United Front (RUF) took over, forcing people to flee their homes and escape to the jungle, heading to wherever they could find shelter. Most of Emma's family ended up in Freetown, the capital of Sierra Leone, but Emma does not know what happened to others, for whom people are still searching.

From her home in the United States, Emma experienced the traumatic effects of the violent conflict indirectly through friends and family in Sierra Leone. Emma tells of how late one night she received a phone call from her sister in Sierra Leone. The family was asleep in their Freetown apartment when somebody knocked on their door. At that time in Sierra Leone, Emma explains, "When you heard a knock late at night, you knew something bad was coming." Her sister told the children to hide under the bed. When the rebels came in they found Emma's thirteen-year old niece and took her with them to carry supplies. Emma's brother-in-law followed them, begging the rebels not to take their daughter. When he started to fight with the rebels he was stabbed in the back with a knife.

Although her brother-in-law survived and her niece was able to escape her captors and return home after two weeks, Emma was deeply affected by their experiences. She said, "I was just crying and yelling, very upset, because, just imagine, it was very, very hard. I said, [to my sister] 'Okay, whatever I can do. I will send some money. I will do what I can to help find her.' I was so upset I didn't go to work. I just prayed, I told my friends the story, they started praying. My sister started talking to people over there, they started praying, the Muslim way, the Christian way, it doesn't matter, they just prayed."

The grief Emma suffered from the loss of friends and family, and her frustration at the barriers to getting aid to the country transformed into social action. She became a leader of the Sierra Leonean community in Portland, working to promote cross-cultural dialogue. She has participated in many activities, including consulting on the documentary video *Diamonds, Guns, and Rice: Sierra Leone and the Women's Peace Movement* and this curriculum.

Section Two: Sierra Leonean Traditions

The idea of this curriculum, *Speaking Out*, began when we visited a refugee camp in Guinea, along the border of Sierra Leone. The women gathered to tell us about their desperate journey out of the war zone. But their talk soon turned to their more immediate worries. While attacks on civilians were less frequent in the relative safety of the refugee settlements, the challenge of finding food and shelter emerged as a more immediate threat to survival. Within weeks of arriving, refugees were expected to establish a means of growing food. Women made use of their traditional secret societies—the social contexts for female initiation rites—to organize and establish community centers and gardens. The women's centers were a hub of activities, from job training, gardening, and dispute resolution, to creating music and theater. Although the secret societies were a mystery to us as outsiders, the women explained that the societies combined traditional practices, such as singing and dancing, with contemporary forms of counseling and discussion groups on gender violence.

Sierra Leoneans, like many other Africans, have preserved cultural practices and modes of work through centuries of colonization and post-colonial domination. However, many traditions have been shaped by the conditions of colonization. The system of chiefdoms, for example, where the "headman" controls the distribution of resources in the village, was strengthened through interactions with colonial powers. Colonial authorities often paid local chiefs to maintain control over local tribal communities and to secure access to resources, such as diamond mines. Yet traditions are not frozen in time. Sierra Leonean traditions, like those practiced elsewhere in the world, do change in response to shifting material conditions and contact with others outside their community. The distance between male and female spheres of work, for example, widen as men leave their villages to find jobs in migratory labor camps. Still other patriarchal traditional practices, such as customary laws granting males control over their female kin, are undermined as women establish networks of female solidarity beyond their local communities and resist patriarchal forms of power.

The crisis of war, along with the devastation and displacements of people, produces opportunities for rebuilding societies. The women refugees with whom we spoke expressed their desire to communicate with people in other countries. More modern technologies, beyond the reach of short wave radios, such as computers and video cameras, were on their list of needs. In videotaping and creating a documentary from the women's stories, we served as their transmission line to parts of the Western world. Their goal was to find resources to create their own transmission lines—means to overcome the isolation and vulnerability they had experienced in their villages. Their challenge, much like that of women elsewhere in the world, centered on the difficult process of separating the sustaining from the destructive elements of cultural practices, and in deciding which traditions to preserve and which to leave behind.

Sierra Leonean traditions provide an important bridge for Western students who may view Sierra Leone as a remote part of the world—and the challenges of its people as incomprehensible. In introducing this culture, we wanted to begin with its vitality. The job of rice farming came to serve as both the symbolic and practical container for this theme. This focus on the sustenance of rice grew out of our discussions with Sierra Leonean women about their traditional roles as farmers, and the connections between West Africa and America established through the slave trade. As Fatima Bona notes in the first section of the documentary, "Rice is the link between us and America." Slaves were captured and brought to the United States for their advanced knowledge of rice farming, and this knowledge contributed, although under the involuntary conditions of slavery, to the early wealth of the United States.

Media portrayals of post-conflict situations offer riveting glimpses of the devastation of war. Simply documenting the scale of horror, however, may inadvertently promote hopelessness about the situation. While not downplaying the scale of the destruction wrought by the Sierra Leonean civil war, our documentary and this curriculum attempted to capture the many remaining human strengths—from innovative approaches to conflict resolution to projects such as interim care centers for ex-combatants and farming cooperatives for women. With the right kind of international assistance, and development practices that include youth and women, communities can flourish in Sierra Leone—one of the poorest and most unstable countries of the world.

In beginning with the rich traditions of Sierra Leone and the cultural practices carried out by women, Section Two establishes a framework for the decade of civil war discussed in Section Three. Opening with a period of tranquility prior to a period of crisis is a conventional technique of storytelling. Our interests go beyond the dramatic arc of the story, however. By focusing on the beauty and vitality of Sierra Leonean culture, we have tried to convey the idea that the atrocities of war are not a natural outgrowth of Sierra Leonean history. Further, this section challenges static definitions of "traditional" and "modern," showing how cultural practices undergo change even in the course of being preserved and transmitted.

This section includes three lessons, all of which take up the role of rice farming in Sierra Leonean culture. Lesson 1, A "Story from Fatima Jarieu Bona," introduces Fatima Jarieu Bona, one of the Sierra Leonean women featured in the documentary *Diamonds, Guns, and Rice: Sierra Leone and the Women's Peace Movement*. Bona tells a childhood story where rice serves as a metaphor for female empowerment. In Lesson 2, "Rice and Sierra Leonean Culture," students watch the first segment of the documentary and explore the role of women in farming in Sierra Leone. Lesson 3, "Sierra Leonean Women and Rice Farming," provides a social history of rice farming as agricultural work and includes a recipe for pap—a traditional rice pudding and staple of the Sierra Leonean diet.

Lesson 1　A Story from Fatima Jarieu Bona

Time: Approximately 50 minutes

Materials:

　Handout: "Fatima Jarieu Bona's Story"

Procedure:

　Distribute "Fatima Jarieu Bona's Story." Ask students to read the interview.

　Divide the class into small discussion groups. Ask each group to select one member to take notes on the group's responses to the following questions:

　　As she grew older, Bona's interpretation of her uncle's story changed. What are two different interpretations? What does each interpretation suggest about the power of men relative to the power of women in Sierra Leone?

　　Bona remembers telling her uncle that his story was "too old." Her uncle replied, "Well, now I know you understand. You know what I want you to be when you grow up." What do you think her uncle was trying to teach her?

　　What might Fatima Bona mean when she concludes that the point of the story is "to hold onto the rice?" What do you think the rice represents in Sierra Leonean culture?

　　Do you agree that the story is outdated or do you think it communicates a message that is still useful? How does the story relate to your own experiences?

　Ask each group to share their responses with the rest of the class.

　Facilitate a class discussion based on themes in the groups' responses.

Homework: Ask students to write a one-page essay describing how Bona's understanding of the story changed, and how her uncle's warning could be interpreted in several ways.

Lesson 2 Rice and Sierra Leonean Culture

Time: Approximately 50 minutes

Materials:

Documentary: Introduction and Part I, "Rice," from *Diamonds, Guns, and Rice* (Cue time: 00:00; Running time: 15:00)

Procedure:

Tell students that Fatima Bona, one of the women featured in the documentary, makes the statement, "Women are the engineers behind farming. Yes, women are the engineers." While watching the documentary, ask students to note ideas or themes in the documentary that might explain this quote. Show the Introduction and Part I, "Rice."

Facilitate a class discussion around the themes and ideas students identify in the documentary and the following questions:

What does rice represent for Sierra Leoneans and their culture, in addition to being the primary food staple?

How has rice production affected Sierra Leonean women and men?

What may rice represent about Sierra Leone, its people, and history?

Homework: Ask students to develop their notes from the class discussion into one-page essays describing the importance of rice in Sierra Leone, including the changing roles of women and men in rice production from pre-colonial times to the present.

Lesson 3   Sierra Leonean Women and Rice Farming

Time: Approximately 50 minutes

Materials:

Handouts: "Rice Farming and Sierra Leonean Culture" and "Making Pap" (used in Homework Option 2)

Procedure:

Distribute "Rice Farming and Sierra Leonean Culture." Explain that students will be asked to respond to questions based on material from the handout. Allow students time to read the essay.

Divide the class into small groups (3–4 students). Assign each group one of the study questions from the essay (listed below). Allow groups time to discuss and write group answers to the following questions:

Why is rice important in Sierra Leone?

How does this essay help to explain Fatima Bona's comment in *Diamonds, Guns, and Rice* that "Rice is the link between us and America"?

What shifts in rice production took place during colonialism? How did these changes affect women and men in Sierra Leone?

How does upland rice compare to swamp rice? What are the benefits and drawbacks of each type? Why would farming households in Sierra Leone prefer to farm upland rice?

Ask volunteers from each group to share their responses with the class. Guide a class discussion based on themes in the students' responses.

Homework Option 1: Ask students to develop their notes from the class discussion into a one-page essay.

Homework Option 2: Distribute "Making Pap" and ask students to read the handout. Students should write a one-page essay responding to the questions below. (Note: Students could earn bonus points for bringing a sample of pap prepared at home to class.)

What is your idea of a traditional American breakfast? How is pap different from the breakfast you described? Is there a cultural difference in the social meaning of pap compared to a traditional American breakfast?

Why is cooking pap considered a skill for Sierra Leonean women? Do you see any differences between the values assigned to women's cooking skills in the U.S. and in Sierra Leone? Explain.

Fatima Jarieu Bona's Story

Fatima Jarieu Bona was born in Freetown, Sierra Leone in 1954. She attended the Freetown Secondary School for Girls and the Saint Helena School. After immigrating to the United States in 1980, Bona received her B.A. in Sociology from Edison College in Trenton, New Jersey. She worked for a number of charity organizations and served as the customer coordinator for Associated Press. Emma lives in Jersey City, New Jersey where she serves as Chairperson for the Sierra Leonean Women's Movement for Peace, member of the African Women's Charity Organization, and Social Secretary for the Sierra Leone American National Association. Bona's greatest aspiration has been to help people.

Bona: We have a tradition that every evening we should all sit around. We sit the children on the floor, the adults sit on a chair, and we tell stories. We tell all kinds of stories before we go to sleep. So during the day, you have to make a story if you don't know one.

Haaken: Do you remember a story that you told, or perhaps a story you heard as a child that stayed with you?

Bona: Yeah, I remember a story. I have an uncle that always gave this story, it could have been for his wife or for women in general. A story about the hen and the rooster. He's trying...now I can tell that he's trying to portray the position of a woman, and where woman should be. You know, he would say, "The hen has rice in her mouth and the rooster was hungry. He wanted that rice in the chicken's mouth, so the rooster said, 'I will talk to her and maybe she will talk, because women talk too much, and if she talks back to me maybe the rice will fall out and I'll pick the rice up and I'll eat it.' But then the rooster did that. He did that for a long time and he talked a storm, but the hen would not take the rice out of her mouth. The rooster said, 'Oh, let me praise her. Let me tell her how beautiful she is. How she can sing. I know women like that.' And then the rooster would do that, started praising the hen and telling the hen how beautiful and how she can sing. And, yes, the hen was like, 'Oh, thank you' and the rice would fall out. And then the rooster

would say 'I know you have a beautiful voice, but you have no common sense.'"

Haaken: Oh!

Bona: That's exactly what he used to say. And I always keep that story now that I'm a woman, because I've analyzed it differently.

Haaken: How do you understand that story?

Bona: I think now he is trying to say that women cannot do, cannot stand up for themselves, cannot hold onto something. A woman cannot speak out, you know, a woman cannot stand up to a man. Men are always, no matter what, they gonna get their way of women. They are going to be coming out on top, they are going to be the successor. You know that's how I feel. That's what I think he was trying to tell us.

Haaken: Was he warning you about this, or was he just saying this is your fate as a woman?

Bona: No, he was warning us. When I grew up, I think there was one time I was old enough and he was saying this story and I said, "You know, this story is too old" and then he said to me, "Well, now I know you understand. You know what I want you to be when you grow up." So I know he was trying to...

Haaken: So he was teaching you something?

Bona: Yes, to hold onto the rice.

Source:

This story was told to Jan Haaken in a videotaped interview for *Diamonds, Guns, and Rice: Sierra Leone and the Women's Peace Movement.*

Rice Farming and Sierra Leonean Culture

Angela Burke

Small, small things have happened to me.
Big, big things have happened to me.
The rice pounder won't see the bottom of the mortar.
(Sande folk song)

Historically, rice has been the most important crop and food source of Sierra Leone. Even if other foods are available, a day would be incomplete without eating rice, either in the form of porridge, or steamed with fish or meat sauce. Because of the importance of rice to daily survival, the people of Sierra Leone have developed a complex cultural identity around rice and rice farming. Cultural life is intertwined with the cycles of farming, and songs are as important a tool as the machete in the production process. Human lives are often measured in relation to the rice crop cycle. For example, Sierra Leoneans often measure the passage of time in relation to the stage of development of the rice crops or the number of crops harvested.

During the Atlantic slave trade, West Africans were valued for their knowledge and skills in rice farming. Slave ships took cargoes of captives from the "Rice Coast" of West Africa to South Carolina in the U.S., where profits from rice plantations created an even greater demand for slave labor. Men were more likely than women to be captured and sold as slaves for foreign markets, resulting in a heavier workload for African women who labored as farmers.

Although Sierra Leonean women marry into patriarchal families, where the husband holds property rights, each wife does have control over a plot of land within the farm. At the time of planting, each farm is divided into areas according to the number of wives in the household. Each wife works with her children to cultivate the rice crop, with men preparing the field for planting (primarily bush clearing) and participating in the final harvest. While the husband controls the crops, the wife keeps control of one of the gardens in her area and is able to sell her crop at a local market.

While the division of labor in Sierra Leone was traditionally organized according to gender, men and women also worked cooperatively. The colonial period, however, introduced capitalist practices into Sierra Leone that divided rice farming into crops produced for local use and those for exchange in foreign markets. These practices also increased the power men asserted over their wives and daughters through customary law. Since crops yielded small surpluses prior to colonial trade practices, farming generated relatively little wealth over which males could assert control. After British colonial rule, however, men gained control over the trade of cash crops, such as palm kernels, cocoa, and coffee. These lucrative crops were more apt to be sold as luxury goods in Western markets. One result of this shift toward cash crops was greater economic dependency of women on men. While women were still farmers, engaged in planting, weeding, and harvesting of rice, male heads of households were the primary beneficiaries of female labor.

The transition to capital-intensive rice farming, with high yield crops produced for foreign markets, also transformed the types of rice that were farmed and the nutritional value of the rice diet.

Two very different kinds of rice are commonly grown in Sierra Leone. The first and preferred type is called upland rice. Upland rice is grown on the hillsides of Sierra Leone. Upland rice farms are only cultivated once every seven years. Unlike industrial farming practices, which use chemicals and produce only one or two crops at a time, Sierra Leonean farmers traditionally have used complex multi-cropping strategies (where many crops are grown together), handed down through generations. By raising rice crops on semi-cleared land, Sierra Leonean farmers can take advantage of the rich fertilizing and pesticide properties of decaying and charred plant debris and avoid using the chemicals and fertilizers necessary for completely cleared land.

In contrast to upland rice, swamp rice, or paddy rice (grown in swamp-like areas) has a much larger crop yield and thus is more likely to be produced as a cash crop for export. Yet swamp rice is not cherished as is upland rice; many Sierra Leoneans find its flavor inferior. Farmers can grow fewer types of crops in these rice paddies than in upland fields. Additionally, swamp rice farming is associated with higher health risks and less overall family benefit than upland rice. During the centuries of slave trade, farming of open, flooded rice patties was very dangerous. Swamp farmers were vulnerable to capture by slave-traders, as well as to other predators.

Unlike the swamps, upland farms provide a protected environment. Because these farming areas are regarded as safe, Sierra Leoneans often retreat upland in times of crisis. The multi-crop method used on upland farms allows family members of different genders, ages, and statuses to participate. Upland farms continue to cultivate a variety of crops, including peppers, beans, corn, cassava, cotton, fruits, and vegetables. While women continue to struggle in a subsistence economy and remain under the control of the male kin, they also hold some authority in these local farming communities. These traditional farming methods have continued despite the pressures to produce cash crops for export rather than production of crops for local use. While some traditions of male control, both customary law and colonial rule, have been oppressive to women as farmers, contemporary Sierra Leonean women farmers do not want to abandon all traditional ways of life.

Sources:

Ferme, M. C. (2001). *The Underneath of Things: Violence, History, and the Everyday in Sierra Leone*. Berkeley, CA: University of California Press.

Richards, P. (1996). *Fighting for the Rain Forest: War, Youth and Resources in Sierra Leone*. London: International African Institute.

Rosen, D. (1983). The Peasant Context of Feminist Revolt in West Africa. *Anthropological Quarterly, 56*, 35–43.

Shaw, R. (2002). *Memories of the Slave Trade: Ritual and Historical Imagination in Sierra Leone*. Chicago: University of Chicago Press.

Shepler, S. (2002). Les Filles-Soldats: Trajectoires d'Apres-Guerre en Sierra Leone [Child Post-War Trajectories for Girls Associated with the Fighting Forces in Sierra Leone]. *Politique Africaine, 21*, 49–62.

Making Pap

Pap, or rice porridge, is made frequently by Sierra Leonean women. It is often eaten for breakfast and is considered a good, soothing base that prepares one for richer foods enjoyed later in the day. This staple is routinely eaten by almost all Sierra Leonean families, but with subtle variations.

In the documentary *Diamonds, Guns, and Rice*, Jariatu Sesay tells how her mother provided for her and her siblings by selling pap. In Sierra Leone, making pap is a time-intensive process. Because of the time involved, not all women prepare pap. Women must first soak the rice, then pound it, and finally steep it in order to obtain the rice flour used in this porridge. Sierra Leonean women have developed the making of this porridge into a craft, with some selling pap to other families in their villages as an economic enterprise.

Emma Fofanah, Cecilia Bangura, and Haja Dukuray passed the following recipe and stories on to us. Mixed in with the recipe and cooking instructions are narrative components provided by these women in a group discussion.

Pap in Sierra Leone is like breakfast. That's what people eat in the morning. It gives you appetite. When you eat pap in the morning, by noon, you know, like by the afternoon, you get really hungry to eat rice.

Mostly if there is a ceremony, like a funeral, you know the fortieth day, they make pap. When someone has a death in the family you call people to pray after the fortieth day somebody died. And then, you know, they will make pap—pap will be served first and then the prayer. And then if somebody has a baby, you know, like a christening, they make pap and then you eat it first before you go to the ceremony—they pass it around. It is just like an appetite for someone to eat more. Also during the month of Ramadan, the Islam holy month, it's the first thing they drink when they break fast to give them appetite. We eat it all year round. During Ramadan if you do that, you make pap, even if you don't fast, it is a blessing to make it to give to those people.

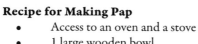

Recipe for Making Pap

- Access to an oven and a stove
- 1 large wooden bowl
- 1 large sauce pan
- 1 cookie sheet
- 1 mixing spoon
- 1 ladle (preferably wood)
- 1 pound rice flour (May be purchased at Asian markets and some health food stores.)
- 2 cups sugar
- 12 and ⅓ cups water, divided
- Juice from 5 limes
- Evaporated milk: 1 can (Optional)
- Tombi (Optional; May be purchased at Asian markets)

Begin by placing all of the rice flour in a mixing bowl (a large calabash is used in Sierra Leone). Measure 1⅓ cups of water. Wet hands and sprinkle water, a small handful at a time, swirling the rice flour as you mix. Mix in circular motions, breaking up the bigger balls until the mixture is the consistency of small curd cottage cheese. As you stir the mixture keep wetting your fingers with water so that the rice flour does not stick to your hands.

In Sierra Leone we use a calabash. The more you hit it against your leg the more you make those little balls.

Optional: Some women dry out the balls before cooking them, others do not. To dry out the mixture, transfer the balls to a cookie sheet and spread them out evenly. Place the cookie sheet in the oven at 200 degrees for ten minutes or until the balls are dry. Stir half way through to keep the balls from sticking.

Back home the women put them in the sun to dry.

The next step works best with two people. Pour eleven cups of water into a large pan and bring to a boil. Reduce to low boil and while one person stirs briskly, the other person drops handfuls of the rice mixture into the water. The balls must cook, which takes about five minutes. The mixture will thicken as it cooks. If the mixture has not reached the desired thickness add 1/4 cup of water to the mixing bowl and swirl it around to get the leftover rice flour from the sides of the bowl. Add this to the pot. It will work as a thickener. Continue to cook the porridge until it is the consistency of a thin pudding.

After the mixture is cooked, add the juice of five medium limes and two cups of sugar (to taste). Cook another 15 minutes or so until the mixture thickens to the consistency of tapioca pudding. (About 15–20 minutes.) If you prefer, you may add a can of evaporated milk. Serve warm for breakfast, with or without milk on the top. Enjoy!

We add fruit, 'tombi,' in it. It is sour. The tombi is brown and gives it a color. It gives pap a flavor and then it gives it a brownish color. Then you put fresh lime. Some people like it sweet. Some people only like it a little sweet so they only put a little bit of sugar. We eat it with milk, then we mix it in. Some people like it really thick, some people like it really thin. It depends how you like it.

Tombi fruit is contained inside a dried pod that looks a bit like a lima bean. Soak the tombi pod to get the fruit. The fruit is then washed and squeezed to remove the seeds, which can be thrown away. The fruit is optional, but most people in Sierra Leone use it. It gives the pap a brown color. Additionally, pap is often eaten with some condensed milk poured over the top. Some people even like to add bits of torn up bread to their porridge.

Section Three:
Globalism and the Economics of the Sierra Leonean Civil War

The Sierra Leonean women (and some men) involved in this project, even as they differed in how to understand the Sierra Leonean conflict, shared the premise that economic factors play a dominant role in warfare. Wars are often fought under the banner of freedom or protection of homeland. Yet outcomes are tallied in economic currencies as much as they are in body count. The currencies involved may be in the form of natural resources, land, or control over capital or labor power.

The hand of the global market increasingly extends its reach. The term globalism refers to the widening interdependence of markets and rapid mobility of labor and capital worldwide, intensified during the last half of the twentieth century through the communications revolution. While globalism creates communication systems that open avenues of progress and cooperation, it also shifts economic powers in ways that marginalize some groups and destroy traditional ways of life. The question is not whether globalism is good or bad, but rather, how human and material resources are used, and what social values guide processes of development. The global justice movement, a term used by many international peace and justice groups, such as World Social Forum, challenges patterns of global capitalism while embracing alternative models of economic development. Rather than focusing on a single issue, global justice activists seek unity around a common set of principles, from environmentalism and fair labor practices to equality for women and minority groups.

In this curriculum guide on women, war, and the global economy, our interest is in making less visible forces operating in the global markets more visible. We wanted to expose the mechanisms of the global economy—the centers of commercial power that, though distant, nonetheless influence the daily lives of people in remote areas of the world. By bringing global economic institutions into focus, Section Three of *Speaking Out* explores how struggles over basic resources—and the institutions that set the terms for those struggles—influence the likelihood of war and the prospects for peace. Bringing the economic context into view need not obscure the cultural, religious, or political dimensions of armed conflict, however. People do fight to defend ideas and principles. Section Three aims to increase students' understanding of how economic factors shape relationships between global economic institutions and developing countries. This framework provides a portal of entry into understanding some of the primary causes of war.

Section Three includes four lesson plans for learning beyond the classroom. Lesson 1, "Cecilia Bangura's Story," draws on the experiences and perspectives of a Sierra Leonean peace activist featured in *Diamonds, Guns, and Rice*. This lesson demonstrates how community activists bring important insights to the discussion of factors underlying war, as well as the how to address them. Through Lesson 2, "Group Relations and the Struggle Over Resources," students learn about colonialism and how its legacy is implicated in the Sierra Leonean civil war. Lesson 3, "Diamonds for Pennies," teaches students about mineral extraction and labor practices associated with the diamond industry. This activity draws on a modified version of the traditional African game Mancala to simulate inequities experienced by Sierra Leonean diamond workers. In Lesson 4, "The Tide of Guns," students learn about connections between the small arms trade and the diamond industry, tracing the flow of small arms in relation to that of diamonds. Each of the first four lessons in this section focuses on a specific party implicated in causing the Sierra Leonean civil war, specified by the Sierra Leonean women who collaborated on this curriculum guide. In Lesson 5, "Complexities of the Sierra Leonean Civil War," students watch Part II of the documentary *Diamonds, Guns, and Rice*, which presents multiple factors underlying the civil war, as emphasized by the women in the documentary. Students learn how these factors are related and have the opportunity to pursue a more nuanced analysis of how diverse factors contribute to armed conflict.

Lesson 1   Cecilia Bangura's Story

Time: Approximately 50 minutes

Materials:

Handouts: "Cecilia Bangura: The International Monetary Fund and World Bank" and Cartoons (three total)

Procedure:

Distribute "Cecilia Bangura: The International Monetary Fund and World Bank." Allow time for students to read the essay.

Facilitate a class discussion based on the following questions:

How does Bangura view the International Monetary Fund (IMF) and World Bank? What are some of the consequences of IMF involvement in Sierra Leone discussed by Bangura (e.g., economic, psychological, for youth, etc.)? In what ways does she criticize international monetary institutions?

In her narrative Bangura tells a story of how, when she was thirsty, the IMF and other global economic institutions "helped" her. What do you think Bangura is saying about effects of the relationship between Sierra Leone and international economic institutions through this story?

In what ways do the IMF and other international economic institutions exert control over developing countries such as Sierra Leone?

According to Bangura, how did international monetary institutions contribute to creating a social context conducive to the outbreak of civil war in Sierra Leone?

Explain to students that they will be creating their own cartoon illustrating their perception of the relationship between Sierra Leone and the IMF and World Bank. Distribute the three Cartoons as examples.

Divide the class into small groups (3–4 students). Ask students to share their perceptions of the impact of global economic institutions on developing nations such as Sierra Leone.

Homework: Ask students to create their own cartoon illustrating their perception of the impact of global economic institutions on Sierra Leoneans. To do so students can draw on what they learned through group discussion, Bangura's narrative, and the themes in the example cartoons. Students also should write a brief description of the commentary illustrated in their cartoon.

Note: Teachers may want to invite students to create posters out of these images, possibly for display in a public area.

Lesson 2   Group Relations and the Struggle Over Resources

Time: Approximately 50 Minutes

Materials:

Handout: "Colonialism and Memory in Sierra Leone"

Procedure:

Distribute "Colonialism and Memory in Sierra Leone." Allow students time to read the handout. Ask them to keep the questions on the handout in mind while reading to prepare for a group discussion.

When students finish reading, divide the class into small groups (3–4 students). Ask groups to discuss the questions on the handout and to be prepared to present their responses to the class.

Ask a volunteer from each group to report the group's responses to the class.

Facilitate a class discussion based on student responses to the discussion questions included in "Colonialism and Memory in Sierra Leone" (listed below):

How are colonialism, neocolonialism, and imperialism different? How are they the same?

What changes took place under colonialism in Sierra Leone? How were women affected by the changes? How were men affected?

Who benefited from the resources in Sierra Leone during colonial times, and what were the resources?

Describe a contemporary example of neocolonialism.

Homework: Ask students to review current media (e.g., newspapers, magazines) and locate an article that discusses an issue related to neocolonialism. Students should write a brief summary of the issue in the article and explain how it relates to neocolonialism. Require students to attach the article to their summary.

Lesson 3   Diamonds for Pennies

Time: Approximately 50 minutes

Note: The game Mancala is readily available for purchase. You may find it at your local non-profit toy store, or you can collect the materials below to assemble it yourself. The game also may be played the traditional way as a cultural exercise. Mancala is appropriate for ages five years through adulthood.

Materials:

> Mancala Boards: These boards consist of two opposing rows of six small bowls. At each end there is a larger bowl, or Kalaha. Students can use empty egg cartons or ice cube trays with a small bowl placed at each end (1 Mancala Board per 4 students)

> Diamonds: Collect marbles, colored candies, dry beans or small stones to represent diamonds (24 diamonds per Diamond Worker, or half the students in the class)

> "Play Money" in increments of 10 cents and $1,000: pennies or tokens to represent increments of 10 cents; pieces of colored construction paper to represent increments of $1,000. (Teachers need an equal amount of Play Money and Diamonds—see Procedure.)

> "Penalty Cards" (1 per Diamond Worker; located with Handouts)

> Handout: "Mancala" (1 per student)

Procedure:

> Explain to students that the game Mancala is played by competing pairs, each of which include a Diamond Worker and a Cartel Partner. Diamond Workers play against each other during the game as Cartel Partners watch. Cartel Partners' role begins after the game ends.

> Divide the class into pairs. Designate one student as the Diamond Worker and the other as the Cartel Partner.

> Assign each pair (Diamond Worker and Cartel Partner) to a competing pair.

> Distribute "Mancala," Mancala Boards (1 per group), and Diamonds (24 to each Diamond Worker). Review the instructions with the students to make sure they understand the game before playing Mancala.

> As students finish playing, distribute a "Penalty Card" to each Diamond Worker and make sure they follow the directions. Also make sure Diamond Workers give their remaining Diamonds to their Cartel Partners.

> Next, ask the Cartel Partners to turn in their Diamonds to the teacher. Explain that the Cartel Partners will receive $1,000.10 for each Diamond, but instruct them to pay their Diamond Workers only 10 cents for each Diamond. Take out the "Play Money," pay the Cartel Partners, and let the Cartel Partners pay the Diamond Workers.

Guide a class discussion based on the following questions:

Why might the team with the most diamonds lose at the end of the game? How does this mirror the situation of Sierra Leoneans?

How did it feel being a Diamond Worker? How did it feel being a Cartel Partner? How did you feel watching the other person in their role?

There are different types and sources of power. Which partner held what kinds of power during the game (e.g., the Cartel Partner held economic power; the Diamond Worker held the power of his labor)? What are other examples of forms of power?

Within the rules there seems to be no way to resist. What would the Diamond Workers have to do to win this game? In the real world, what forms of resistance could the diamond workers engage in?

In Western culture diamonds generally are viewed as a valuable commodity. Did the experience of playing this game change students' perceptions of diamonds' value?

Homework: Ask students to choose a diamond ad from a magazine or newspaper and modify it to communicate an alternate message. Explain that "alternate" means different from what was intended by the advertiser. To modify the ad students may (a) illustrate their own version or (b) cut, draw on, write on, or otherwise physically alter the ad itself after photocopying the original. Ask students to provide a brief explanation of the intended meaning of the original ad, the alternate message in their version and how these contrast. Students should turn in both ads with the explanation.

Lesson 4   The Tide of Guns

Time: Approximately 50 minutes

Materials:

Overhead: "World Map"

Handouts: "Small Arms: The Real Weapons of Mass Destruction?," "World Map," and "Tracing the Trail of Diamonds"

Procedure:

Prior to the day of class, distribute "Small Arms: The Real Weapons of Mass Destruction?" Ask students to read the essay in preparation for the activity and to pay particular attention to the trail of arms described in the reading. Explain to students that they will use this information to map sources and destinations of small arms onto a map of the world.

Distribute "World Map" and "Tracing the Trail of Diamonds."

Divide the class into small groups (3–4 students). Alert students that they will have a writing assignment that draws on the group discussion. Ask groups to read the handouts, discuss the trail of small arms depicted in the essay, and map the trail onto their world map. In preparation for the writing assignment, groups should discuss the following questions:

How do the diamond industry and small arms trade overlap? What are some similarities and differences between the flow of diamonds as shown in "Tracing the Trail of Diamonds" and the flow of arms as indicated in their own maps?

What roles do the diamond industry and small arms trade play in the Sierra Leonean civil war?

How do these industries affect ordinary people in Sierra Leone?

Homework: Ask students to write a one-page response to the questions above. Student responses can draw on the essay, maps, and group discussion.

Lesson 5   Complexities of the Sierra Leonean Civil War

Time: Approximately 50 minutes

Materials:

Documentary: Part II, "Guns and Diamonds," from *Diamonds, Guns, and Rice* (Cue time: 14:50; Running time: 17:00) (Note: If students have not seen the Introduction and Part I, teachers may want to show the documentary from the beginning.)

Handout: "Factors Underlying the Sierra Leonean Civil War"

Procedure:

Distribute "Factors Underlying the Sierra Leonean Civil War." Review the questions with the students.

Show Part II, "Guns and Diamonds," from *Diamonds, Guns, and Rice.*

Divide the class into small groups (3–4 students). Ask students to discuss, and develop, their answers to the questions on the handout.

Facilitate a class discussion based on group responses to the questions included in "Factors Underlying the Sierra Leonean Civil War."

Homework: Ask student to write a one-page essay addressing the two following questions:

Describe one image, scene, or story in the documentary that influenced your understanding of the causes of the Sierra Leonean civil war.

Why do you think this segment impacted your perceptions of the war?

Cecilia Bangura: The International Monetary Fund and World Bank

Cecilia Bangura was born in Senjehune, a village in the Bunthe district of Sierra Leone. This district is in the Southern province, which is predominantly Mende (one of the primary ethnic groups of Sierra Leone). She came from a polygamous home; her father was a paramount chief and had a wife in each section of the chiefdom. There was a mix of religions in her childhood home: her mother's family was Muslim while her father's family was Christian and Muslim. She lived as a Muslim in the village with her aunt, studying Arabic until the age of five, when she left the village to live with her sister in Freetown, attending Catholic school and studying English. She continued there through the 12th grade and then spent two years attending college on the East coast of the United States. When her money ran out she returned to Freetown, where she stayed until after she was married. She returned to the United States five months pregnant and with a two-year-old in May 1992 to join her husband, and has not returned to Sierra Leone since. Although she did not leave Sierra Leone because of the war, it had already started when she left, and was escalating in the countryside. Bangura now resides with her husband and three daughters in Portland, Oregon, where she is a leader and peace activist in the Sierra Leonean community. She has served as an officer in the Northwest Sierra Leonean Association. Bangura agreed to be interviewed for the documentary Diamonds, Guns, and Rice, *as well as to take on a consultation role, and to participate in developing the curriculum guide* Speaking Out.*

In an interview focused on causal factors in the Sierra Leonean civil war, Ariel Ladum asks Bangura about her views on the effects of the relationship between global economic institutions, such as the International Monetary Fund (IMF) and World Bank, and Sierra Leoneans, and how criteria imposed by these institutions as conditions for receiving loans contributed to the outbreak of civil war.

Bangura: I do not know who those international monetary organizations are working for, or what they are working for, but they are not working for the human being. They say they are gonna come help you, "O.K. Cecilia, I'll help you by giving you this aid if you cut this or you stop that." They make me do everything against my development! It's like you say to them, "I'm thirsty," and they say back to you, "O.K., if you get rid of your saliva, your spittle, I'll give you water." Heh! Dehydrate myself thoroughly before I get help! I could at least gather that saliva and send it down to at least wet my parched throat. I do not have to spit my saliva out so you can give me water. Add water to my saliva, it can obviously quench my thirst or solve the purpose for which I need water. But "get rid of that and I'll give you this" finds me worse off. And not only that, I have to give you back your water! It's not only the few ounces you give me—if you give me two ounces I have to give you seven ounces back. Are you really looking out for me? No. That is the way I look at it.

Before devaluation, the Leone and cents (the national currency) were not only at par, they were stronger than the dollar. Our currency was the biggest thing going for us—Sierra Leoneans were happy and living well. But the IMF demanded devaluation of our currency, and we suffered so many other things. So devaluation comes and the Leone plummets. After devaluation you don't want the Leone even in Sierra Leone. I want pound sterling, I want dollar, I want the stronger currencies. That affected a lot. If you went to go rent a home you could not get decent housing because everybody wanted pound sterling and dollars for rent money. We don't have the hotels being full now because people have to pay in dollars or pound sterling. You cannot go check in for a weekend break or anything if you don't have foreign currency. There was no access to facilities or services for local people. The young generation, the young people, were left with nothing to do. They have all this energy, all these possibilities, all this potential, with nothing. No infrastructure, no nothing. Satan finds some mischief for idle hands to do, you know.

The devaluation of our currency was the first movement that led to all of this suffering and is still killing us. It is an economic situation that just isn't working. All this emptiness in so many people's lives who really shared the experience of this war—there was nothing for all these young people to do so they got attracted easily and they're easily sucked into all this fighting. These economic institutions are not looking out for the human, you know, the people they say they are going to help. They want so much out of the country—grab, grab, grab—and you must pay back this loan they give.

by Tom Lechner

Colonialism and Memory in Sierra Leone

Jan Haaken

Keep the following questions in mind while reading the essay:

How are colonialsm, neocolonialism, and imperialism different? How are they the same?

What changes took place under colonialism in Sierra Leone? How were women affected by the changes? How were men affected?

Who benefited from the resources in Sierra Leone during colonial times, and what were the resources?

Describe a contemporary example of neocolonialism.

In *Memories of the Slave Trade: Ritual and the Historical Imagination in Sierra Leone*, anthropologist Rosalind Shaw describes how images of colonial conquest are preserved through rituals, legends, and the mapping of the physical boundaries. Based on field research carried out in Sierra Leone in the 1980s and 90s, Shaw shows how beliefs in, for example, the sudden seizure of humans by malevolent spirits, register the history of the slave raids that continued in Sierra Leone long after the British outlawed the slave trade. Present difficulties, Shaw explains, re-vitalize traumatic images from the past. Previous forms of domination are brought to life by contemporary forms of exploitation in Sierra Leone, serving as cautionary tales. Shaw recounts, for example, rumors circulating in Sierra Leone in the 1980s of politicians secretly practicing cannibalism—rumors that Shaw interprets as symbolic ways of expressing outrage against elected officials who "cannibalize" the country's resources.

Looking back on the history of colonialism through the lens of folk culture, Shaw notes various risks of misinterpretation. There may be only a tenuous correspondence, for instance, between the legends a society produces and the actual events that may have given rise to that legend. But Shaw attempts to show how colonized peoples often preserve and transmit history in ways that are not readily accessible to outsiders.

There are key historical events that are widely recognized as important markers, however, in Sierra Leonean history. Many of these events mark the upheavals associated with colonial domination of Sierra Leone and are an important context for understanding the civil war of the 1990s. Colonialism refers to a system of domination whereby a foreign power rules a country or region by establishing administrative control over its political, economic, and cultural life. Whereas imperialism involves domination through foreign policy or trade, colonialism entails more intimate forms of power. Settlers from the colonizing country govern indigenous peoples in ways that shape the daily lives and psychological identities of those people, from daily habits concerning time and cleanliness to cultural and spiritual practices. There are different expressions and patterns of colonialism, just as there are differing accommodations and resistances to colonial rule.

The colony of Sierra Leone grew out of a complex mix of humanistic and exploitative interests. Formed by British abolitionists and philanthropists in the late eighteenth century as a refuge for escaped slaves, the province of Freetown was established in 1787 as a British Crown colony. In the late eighteenth and early nineteenth centuries, hundreds of American blacks joined escaped and freed slaves from Britain, Nova Scotia, and various regions of Africa in the new settlement. Some support for the "back to Africa" campaign grew out of white racist fears of these now uncontrollable blacks. Many abolitionists charged that the campaign perpetuated the racist idea that freed blacks could not be integrated into European societies. Others, including many black abolitionists, saw in the colonization campaign a means of reversing some of the traumatic losses suffered by blacks through the Atlantic slave trade. Much like Liberia, established by the American Colonization Society in 1821 as a colony for escaped slaves, Sierra Leone was thought to reflect the moral capacity of European conquerors to make reparations for the slave trade. Many of the philanthropic efforts focused on the ideal of literacy for African blacks. Fourah Bay College, established in Freetown by the British in 1827, rapidly became the largest and most prestigious English-speaking sub-Saharan university.

When we move from this beacon of enlightenment to the more shadowy side of colonial history, a disturbing picture emerges of Sierra Leone's colonial past. The settlement established in 1787 for freed slaves overturned earlier agreements between European traders and local Temne chiefs concerning use of land. Once the chiefs recognized that the British had established a permanent colony, the settlement was burned to the ground. The Sierra Leone Company, a London-based corporation, assumed control of the land in 1791 and named the reconstructed settlement Freetown. In 1808, however, after the Sierra Leone Company collapsed due to financial losses, the British government took over and installed a British governor to rule the area, forcibly annexing Temne land, driving Temnes inland.

Although the British made slave trading illegal in 1806, the British allowed slavery to continue in rural areas for another century. Further, the "legitimate" trade promoted through colonial expansion bordered on slavery. Blacks labored on colonial farms under slave-like conditions for less than subsistence wages. Further, the increased European and American demands for luxury goods—coffee, sugar, cocoa, and later diamonds—intensified the economic dependency of colonizers on cheap labor. Slave raiding intensified in Sierra Leone and Guinea in the nineteenth century, as did smuggling of slaves into the colonial farms.

Colonial development of Sierra Leone also created deep enmity between Creoles (or Krios), the English-speaking immigrants from Britain and America, and indigenous ethnic groups. As the primary ethnic group in newly established Freetown, Krios were granted a privileged status in administering the colony. In the rural areas, some black African traders also amassed wealth through trade, including the slave trade. Under the chiefdom system, Paramount Chiefs were granted enhanced authority in overseeing extraction of rich mineral deposits, which became the basis for exports. During colonialism, many men, unable to survive on subsistence farming, joined labor camps where they worked in the mines under slave-like conditions.

After the British initiated a rail system in 1895 to bring remote areas into trade networks, the British formally annexed the rural Mende (one of the two largest ethnic groups in Sierra Leone) territory into Sierra Leone as a protectorate. Taxes were imposed by the British administration on villages, which led to a bloody insurrection. The British responded quickly and brutally, publicly executing Mende fighters.

The railway system followed a course of progress charted by the colonial powers, built through the forced labor of rural people. Yet in 1920, Sierra Leonean railway workers went on strike and formed a union, ushering in a period of radicalization and anti-colonial struggle.

From tribal chiefs and colonial bosses through modern corporations and banks, power involves the creation of dependency. Those who control wealth—whether measured in land, cattle, or capital—are in a position to create subjects, those without wealth who are placed in a position of dependency. The violence of colonial trade in Sierra Leone, like other areas of Africa, strengthened patriarchal authority over women. Threats from slave traders and colonial conquest intensified female reliance on men for protection, but at the same time these threats also created female enclaves and secret societies beyond the direct control of men.

Britain, the dominant European colonial power throughout the nineteenth century, relinquished control over most of its colonies, including Sierra Leone, in the decades following the Second World War. Relinquishment of power was a response to organized political and armed resistance rather than a result of moral enlightenment. Sierra Leone gained independence from Britain in 1961, but the lasting repercussions of colonialism still plague its people. As Jariatu Sesay states in the documentary *Diamonds, Guns,* *and Rice*, "Sierra Leone may be independent, but we are still colonized—intellectually, we are still colonized."

Colonialism persists on psychological as well as material levels. Franz Fanon, the anti-colonial psychiatrist writing in the context of the Algerian independence movement, described the ways in which colonized peoples often identify with their colonizers. Fanon and other post-colonial writers explain how colonized peoples often displace their hostility toward their oppressors onto others among the oppressed. In a defense described as identification with the aggressor, the individual asserts control by attacking more vulnerable members of the group because an individual lacks control in relation to the oppressor. Rather than joining together to fight the oppressors, the oppressed turn their aggression inward against those within their own community.

Although colonization has ended, its traumatic effects may be perpetuated through processes of neocolonialism. Unlike colonialism, neocolonialism does not involve the actual presence of foreign administrators. Although the developing country may enjoy political independence, a more powerful nation (often the former colonizer) retains control through indirect means such as economic, financial, and trade policies. Less brutal and direct in its effects than colonial domination, neocolonialism (or what some term imperialism) can be equally devastating for developing nations. It operates through institutions of globalization, including transnational corporations and international economic institutions such as the International Monetary Fund (IMF), World Trade Organization, and World Bank. These organizations share the goals of integrating developing countries into global markets—goals that carry some of the same colonial impulses of former eras. Developing nations (along with Western critics of the globalization process) may see little difference between colonialism as practiced in the nineteenth and early twentieth centuries and neocolonialism in its present manifestation. In effect, the results are similar—the exploitation of the developing world's resources and peoples. Just as colonial domination generated forms of resistance and the eventual overthrow of colonial rule, globalism has generated new forms of opposition. Whether more equitable patterns of development emerge depends on the ability of new generations to imagine alternatives to the colonial past.

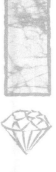

Sources:

Adebajo, A. (2002). *Building Peace in West Africa: Liberia, Sierra Leone, and Guinea-Bissau.* Boulder, CO: Lynne Rienner Publishers.

Fanon, F. (1986; 1952). *Black Skin, White Masks.* London: Pluto.

_____ (1990; 1963). *The Wretched of the Earth.* London: Penguin.

Keene, D. (2003). Greedy Elites, Dwindling Resources, Alienated Youths: The Anatomy of Protracted Violence in Sierra Leone. International Politics and Society, 2. Retrieved July 2005 from http://fesportal.fes.de/pls/portal30/docs/FOLDER/IPG/IPG2_2003/ARTKEEN.HTM

Rashid, Ismail. (1999). "Do Dady nor Lef me Make dem Carry me": Slave resistance and emancipation in Sierra Leone, 1894–1928. In Susanne Miers and Martin Klein (Eds.). *Slavery and Colonial Rule in Africa.* Portland, OR: Frank Cass, 208–231.

Rosen, D. M. (1983). The Peasant Context of Feminist Revolt in West Africa. *Anthropological Quarterly* 56(1), 35–43.

Shaw, R. (2002). *Memories of the Slave Trade: Ritual and the Historical Imagination in Sierra Leone.* Chicago: University of Chicago Press.

Mancala

Historians believe that Mancala, a traditional African game, is the oldest game in the world. Children and adults in most African countries enjoy some version of Mancala. In some African villages Mancala may be used as a ceremonial rite of passage, in others simply a form of recreation. It may be played on elaborate playing boards or by digging a few simple holes in the ground and using pebbles as game pieces.

The game Mancala is played by competing pairs. In this version, one person in each pair is the Diamond Worker and the other is the Cartel Partner. Diamond Workers represent the people doing the manual labor in diamond mining. Cartel Partners represent the business agents of the large diamond companies. During the game Diamond Workers from competing pairs are opponents. Cartel Partners advise their Diamond Worker counterparts while they play against each other. If there is a dispute over a maneuver, the Cartel Partner has the power to override the Diamond Worker throughout the game. The Cartel Partner takes over when the Diamond Workers finish playing Mancala.

The Diamond Workers start out with six bowls of diamonds. Throughout the game Diamond Workers may move any diamond on their side of the board, but they may not move diamonds on their opponent's side. Mancala ends when all six bowls of either player are empty. The player with diamonds remaining in their bowls puts them into their Kalaha— one of the two larger bowls at each end of the board. The object of the game is to end up with the most diamonds in the Kalaha.

Directions

Place the Mancala Board on a flat surface between you. Take 24 diamonds each and put four in each of the six bowls on your side of the board. Do not put any in your Kalaha. These must be empty at the start of the game.

Starting the Game: If you are first, scoop all the diamonds from any bowl on your side of the board. Moving to the right, drop one diamond into each bowl. If you come to your Kalaha, drop in one diamond. If you still have Diamonds continue dropping them into bowls on your opponent's side, but skip their Kalaha.

Taking an Additional Turn: You may go again if your last diamond lands in your own Kalaha. Otherwise, it becomes your opponent's turn when you run out of the Diamonds you scooped from the bowl.

Capturing Your Opponents Diamonds: If the last diamond you drop goes into an empty bowl on your side of the board, you capture your opponent's diamonds in the bowl directly across from yours by putting them in your Kalaha. It becomes your opponent's turn after you make a capture.

End of Game: The game ends when all six bowls belonging to either Diamond Worker are empty. The Diamond Worker whose diamonds remain in the bowls moves them to their Kalaha. At this time each Diamond Worker receives a Penalty Card, follows the directions, and then turns over their remaining diamonds to their Cartel Partner. Next, Cartel Partners turn the diamonds in to the teacher for payment in Play Money and wait for directions from the teacher.

Penalty Cards

You have a family to care for and must take time out to look for food.

Lose ½ of your diamonds. Turn ½ over to your Cartel Partner.

You were captured and forced to work as a slave mining diamonds. You escaped but with only 2 diamonds.

Lose all but 2 diamonds. Turn the 2 diamonds over to your Cartel Partner.

You were attacked by rebels and lost an arm. You can't work as quickly as the other diamond workers.

Lose all but ⅓ of your diamonds. Turn your remaining ⅓ over to your Cartel Partner.

You were captured and forced to work as a slave mining diamonds. You have found many diamonds but cannot keep any.

Lose all your diamonds. Explain to your Cartel Partner that you have no diamonds.

You are a local chief. In return for controlling the youth in your village you are entitled to half of all mined diamonds.

Keep all your diamonds and take ½ of *every other* Diamond Worker's remaining diamonds. Turn over all the diamonds to your Cartel Partner.

You are hired as a guard for the mines. Your village shuns you because of your position and you are not allowed to keep any diamonds from the mines.

Turn all your diamonds over to your Cartel Partner and wait for your daily pay of 10 cents.

Small Arms: The Real Weapons of Mass Destruction?

Thomas Becker

Thomas Becker is retired from the electrical trade. He presently does commentary and reporting on KBOO radio and has written for the Portland Alliance.

While most of world, particularly the U.S., remains obsessed with the control of weapons of mass destruction (nuclear, biological, and chemical), our planet also is awash in another deadly scourge of weapons that seems to have gone relatively unnoticed. By current estimates, there are some 500 million to one billion small arms circulating the globe and contributing to political and social instability in many areas of the world such as the Balkans, the former Soviet Republics, Latin America and the continent of Africa.

Small arms may be loosely defined as any weapon that is portable by humans or pack animals and can be fired by a single individual or a small team of individuals working in tandem. In addition to handguns and rifles, this category includes automatic rifles, machine guns, grenades, land mines, and shoulder fired anti-aircraft and anti-tank missiles.

Corinne Dufka, a senior researcher and the West Africa Team Leader of the Africa Division of Human Rights Watch, was based in Freetown, Sierra Leone, from 1999 to 2003. In her testimony before the U.S. House International Relations Committee on combating war crimes in Africa in June 2004, Dufka succinctly defined the ongoing proliferation of small arms in West Africa and the horrendous results.

Africa is a sad showcase of the human rights and humanitarian costs of the uncontrolled proliferation of small arms and light weapons. Quantities of arms have flowed to the region causing the rampant misuse of such weapons by state and non-state actors alike. The easy availability of small arms, conflict, and human rights abuses in West Africa are interwoven. The spread and misuse of small arms helps fuel conflict, and conflict generates a market for more weapons. These weapons, in the hands of combatants who have a history of indifference for the principle of civilian immunity, lead to grave violations against innocent people. Mercenaries and arms traffickers make a tidy profit off their trades, and the combatants can often count on outside support to finance their wars. But, it is civilians who ultimately pay the highest price.

It is estimated that small arms cause some 365,000 deaths worldwide on an annual basis.[1] Most of these deaths occur in third world war zones such as Sierra Leone, Congo, Angola, Sri Lanka, and Columbia.

According to the 1994 Yearbook of the Stockholm International Peace Institute, "all 34 of the major armed conflicts underway in 1993 were intrastate conflicts, involving combat between state security forces and antigovernment insurgents or among competing ethnic, religious, and tribal militias... [These forces] are normally equipped with whatever arms they can carry with them or transport into an area using pack animals, or light aircraft and vehicles."[2] The United Nations estimates that small arms were the principle weapons in 46 of the 49 conflicts that erupted in the 90s.[3] And more recently, in July 2001, the U.S. government estimated that "small arms are fueling conflicts in 22 African countries that have taken 7–8 million lives."[4]

As horrific as these numbers are, they do not begin to tell the tragic dimensions of small arms proliferation and the wars these small arms are fuelling. It is well documented that in these third world war zones, civilian deaths far outnumber those of the combatants, and consist mostly of women and children. By way of comparison, it is estimated that in World War I civilian casualties accounted for 5 percent of total casualties. In these more recent wars, they account for some 90 percent.

Child soldiering is yet another tragic component of small arms proliferation. According to UN estimates, "There are more than 300,000 children in government armies, rebel forces, and guerrilla groups in more than 30 countries, including at least 5,000 child soldiers in Sierra Leone." The methods of recruitment of these child soldiers are as varied as they are brutal, involving intimidation and threats, beatings, bribery, drugging, and outright kidnapping. Orphaned children often see joining armies as the only means of survival—at the least they can hope for some protection within the group, as well as being fed and clothed.

Child soldiers are attractive to both government militias and insurgency groups for more cynical reasons than their ready availability. Children are perceived as small and speedy, easy to intimidate, economically exploitable, and less likely to rebel. Small arms and light weapons are easy to handle and maintain. A child can be taught to use them to deadly effect with minimal training. Fueled on drugs and visions of Rambo-like invincibility, they can be deluded into a fevered conviction of their own indestructibility and can be sent as fodder into the most dangerous sections of a battle. Deceived into thinking of war as a game, some children kill and maim without conscience

1 Annan, K. (July 9, 2001). *Small Arms, Big Problems.* Speech before The United Nations Conference on the Illicit Trade in Small Arms and Light Weapons in All Its Aspects.

2 Klare, M.T. (Sept. 22, 1995). Stemming the Lethal Trade in Small Arms and Light Weapons. *Issues in Science and Technology.*

3 Bondi, L. (2002). Disillusioned NGOs Blame the United States for a Weak Agreement. *SAIS Review. 22*(1).

4 Fleshman, M. (Dec. 2001). Small Arms in Africa: Counting the Cost of Gun Violence. *Africa Recovery. 15*(4).

or discretion. (One of the agonies in Sierra Leone is the attempt to reintegrate these brutalized and consequently often brutal children back into their communities—some of whom once waged war on their own villages.)

Where are all the weapons coming from? The general flow is from the more industrially developed countries of the world to the less developed, unstable areas of the world. In recent years, the United States is responsible for supplying small arms to 16 of the 18 countries in which small arms conflicts are a destabilizing influence. Although led by the U.S., many other countries, including those of the European Union, are involved in the manufacturing of small arms and light weapons. The UN Institute for Disarmament has identified nearly 300 companies operating in 52 nations that are involved in the manufacture of small arms.

Another major source for weapons is the former Soviet Union. Russia is awash in an excess of AK-47s and other small arms since the disintegration of the Soviet Union in 1989. Profiteering soldiers, from generals to privates, are selling these weapons on the black market. The AK-47 is also currently under manufacture in many other countries besides the former Soviet Union, including China, Egypt, Finland, Hungary, North Korea, Poland, Romania, and Yugoslavia. This manufacturing is done either through legitimate licensing agreements or by "reverse engineering"—disassembling a sample to see how it is made.

Although supplied by many countries of the world, the sale of small arms and light weapons falls into three categories. First are "legitimate" sales or transfers from government to government or from government to insurgency group. A telling example is the U.S. arming of the Taliban during Afghanistan's war with Russia, and later arming the Northern Alliance when the Taliban turned against the U.S. disproving the old adage that "the enemy of my enemy is my friend." Second, legally sanctioned sales from private manufacturers to governments or insurgency groups contribute significantly to the vast proliferation of small arms. While this area is the most closely monitored and controlled type of sale, it is certainly an important player in the escalating violence of wars fought with small arms. Last is the black market operated by illegal traffickers and criminal gangs. This area is the most difficult to monitor and control, and where most current attention is focused. One must keep in mind, however, that every "legitimate" gun sold has the strong possibility of winding up on this illegal market at some point. If any progress is to be made in ending or significantly reducing the illicit small arms trade, it must begin by reducing, regulating, and strictly controlling the "legitimate" trade.

Since the collapse of the Soviet Union in 1989, bringing an end of the cold war, government transfers of small weapons have been in steady decline. It is fair to say that those in the market for weapons today are going to have to pay for them. But most of these weapons wind up in countries that are extremely poor, such as Sierra Leone. Where

does the money come from to purchase all this weaponry? These weapons are relatively inexpensive and a few million dollars can go a long way. The weapons market is financed through activities such as drug smuggling and plundering of precious stones and minerals by governments and insurgency groups alike.

In Sierra Leone diamonds are the principal source of revenue. These stones, when mined and sold by rebel or insurgency groups, are described as dirty diamonds, conflict diamonds, or blood diamonds. The United Nations, the concerned governments, and peace and justice oriented NGOs (nongovernmental organizations)—such as the International Action Network on Small Arms which is an umbrella group consisting of over 200 organizations—are working to prevent the trafficking of these illicit diamonds to buy weapons. As important as restricting this traffic is, it should be noted that when "legitimate" governments, no matter how corrupt and tyrannical, mine and sell these diamonds they are "clean." But don't be fooled—the profits are just as likely to go towards the purchase of weapons. No matter who is buying and selling, one thing remains constant—the people of Sierra Leone, as elsewhere, reap no benefit, only more violence and misery.

In 2001, the United Nations turned its full attention to the massive and continually escalating traffic in death and human misery caused by small arms. In July of that year and running for 11 days, the United Nations Conference on the Illicit Trade in Small Arms and Light Weapons in All its Aspects took place in New York City. (The word "illicit" being something of a misnomer as the Conference sought for more effective methods to monitor and control the legal trade as well.) From the very beginning, hopes were dashed that a meaningful program of action would emerge from these sessions. While a world leader in unilateral legislation and bilateral agreements regarding the sale and transport of small arms, the United States made its position clear that it would not accept any binding multilateral agreements to emerge from these sessions.

To the dismay of most other nations, the U.S. put forth a document of non-negotiable demands that scuttled any hope of an agreement with enforcement provisions, citing such reasons as infringement on its national sovereignty, protecting the U.S. small arms industry, and the principle of free enterprise. The obstructionist position of the U.S. came as no surprise to the other participants. The present U.S. government has been ideologically consistent in opposing any agreement that calls for multilateral cooperation. Perhaps most dismaying was the U.S. position on the attempt to ban the use of child soldiers—those under 18 years of age. U.S. recruiting policy allows seventeen year old children to enlist in the military with parental consent. Although the U.S. acknowledges that only approximately 3,000 such soldiers in a military force of some 1.2 million

are on active duty at any one time, issues of national sovereignty were considered to be of higher priority as the U.S. elected not to support the ban on child soldiering.

NGOs and many foreign governments continue organizing to combat the plague of small arms proliferation. Hundreds of concerned NGOs attended the UN conference in 2001 and are increasing their efforts to advocate and lobby for this cause. One goal is to link the issue of small arms proliferation directly to one of human rights. This was the successful strategy that led to the Ottawa Treaty to ban land mines worldwide—in spite of the "no" vote of the U.S. delegation.

An outright ban on small arms is problematic, however. Governments have a right to protect their sovereignty, and when governments are oppressive and arbitrary, insurgency groups may claim the right of armed resistance—witness the American Revolution as one example. Nevertheless, many groups throughout the world are deeply concerned about the growing proliferation of small arms and are committed to limiting, controlling and reducing their number.

A simple reduction in the quantity of weapons available to combatants is only part of what is needed to alleviate intrastate conflicts and the levels of violence they engender. In an unjust world of inequitable resource distribution, more systemic changes need to take place, changes that thrust ultimate responsibility directly on the U.S., the European Union (EU) and other developed nations.

Forgiving the massive debts incurred by developing countries through large scale lending from the World Bank and the International Monetary Fund seems an obvious first step. Throughout the periods of colonialism and imperialism[1] continuing to the present day, the West has exploited the underdeveloped world's natural and human resources through slavery and wage exploitation.

Equally important would be the restructuring of International Monetary Fund (IMF) and World Bank policies towards internal economic development and improvement in standards of living for developing countries. Instead, under current policy poor countries are forced to submit to the dictates of the global market where their floundering economies are subject to further exploitation and degradation.

Stopping or slowing the proliferation of small arms must be understood as one component of a much broader program of action. Lasting progress requires the coupling of this effort with efforts to address underlying structural problems of resource redistribution and building sustainable economies. As long as chronic illness, hunger, hopelessness, and abject poverty are the lot of so many, continued violence and, consequently, the demand for small arms have little chance of abating

---

1 Colonialism and imperialism often go undifferentiated. Although closely related, there are readily identifiable differences. In colonialism, a huge administrative bureaucracy is established by the colonizing country within the colonized country to run all its affairs—government, law, taxation, police, military, and other such functions. Mass migrations of people from the "mother" country to the colonized country may also occur. The colonizing country openly declares its sovereignty over the colonized. Imperialism presents a more subtle face. While the subjected country may appear autonomous and even have some degree of autonomy, its economic life and governmental policies (especially, foreign policy) are forced into subservience to the imperial power through economic trade policies. In general it may be said that the era of colonialism is at an end and that the era of imperialism is ongoing.

Sources:

Annan, K. (July 9, 2001). Small Arms, Big Problems. Speech before The United Nations Conference on the Illicit Trade in Small Arms and Light Weapons in All Its Aspects.

Anonymous. (Dec. 4, 2002). Biggest Terror Threat is Small Arms. *Christian Science Monitor*.

BBC News. (Nov. 21, 2001). Child Soldier Asks UN for Help. Retrieved from http://news.bbc.co.uk/hi/english/world/africa

Bondi, L. (2002). Disillusioned NGOs Blame the United States for a weak agreement. *SAIS Review*, 22(1), 229–233.

Bonner, R. (July 13, 1998). 21 Nations Seek to Limit the Traffic in Small Arms. *The New York Times*.

Cook, R. (Mar. 20, 2001). Regulating and Reducing the Scourge of Small Arms. *The Independent* (Bangladesh)

Editorial desk. (July 11, 2001). An American Retreat on Small Arms. *The New York Times*.

Fleshman, M. (Dec. 2001). Small Arms in Africa: Counting the cost of gun violence. *Africa Recovery*, 15(4).

Human Rights Watch. (January 17, 2000). United States Opposition Jeopardizes Global Ban on Child Soldiers. Children's Rights: *HRW World Report 2000.* Retrieved from http://www.hrw.org/press/2000.

Klare, M. (Sept. 22, 1995). Stemming the Lethal Trade in Small Arms and Light Weapons. *Issues in Science and Technology*.

Klare, M. (Jan./Feb., 1999). The Kalashnikov Age. *Bulletin of the Atomic Scientists*, 55(1).

Renner, M. (Jan./Feb., 1999). Arms Control Orphans. *Bulletin of the Atomic Scientists*, 55(1).

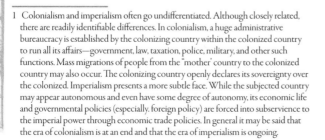

Physical Map of the World

Map courtesy of the University of Texas

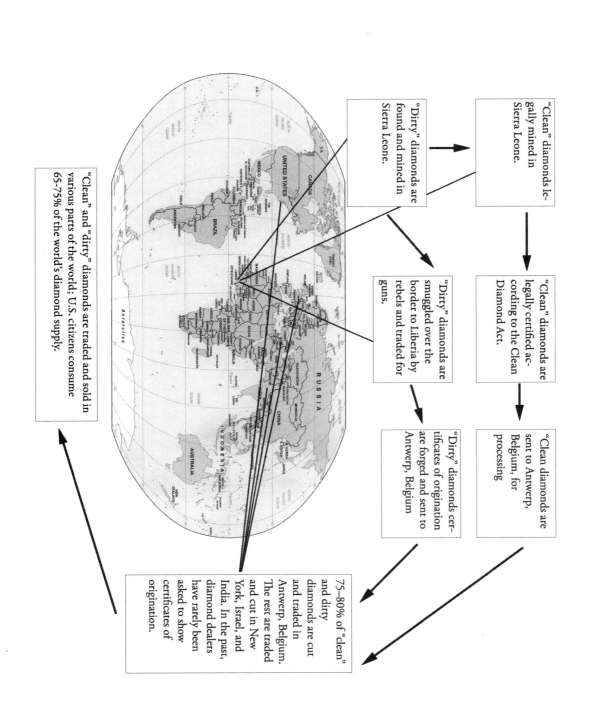

"Clean" diamonds legally mined in Sierra Leone.

"Dirty" diamonds are found and mined in Sierra Leone.

"Clean" diamonds are legally certified according to the Clean Diamond Act.

"Dirty" diamonds are smuggled over the border to Liberia by rebels and traded for guns.

"Clean diamonds are sent to Antwerp, Belgium, for processing

"Dirty" diamonds certificates of origination are forged and sent to Antwerp, Belgium

75–80% of "clean" and dirty diamonds are cut and traded in Antwerp, Belgium. The rest are traded and cut in New York, Israel, and India. In the past, diamond dealers have rarely been asked to show certificates of origination.

"Clean" and "dirty" diamonds are traded and sold in various parts of the world; U.S. citizens consume 65-75% of the world's diamond supply.

Factors Underlying the Sierra Leonean Civil War

As you watch Part II, "Guns and Diamonds," from *Diamonds, Guns, and Rice*, take notes on the following:

1) The women interviewed in the documentary emphasize diverse factors in causing the Sierra Leonean civil war:

> Some factors are more contemporary while others have a historical basis. Give an example of each.

> Some factors relate to Sierra Leonean culture while others have a more economic basis. Give an example of each.

> Some factors implicate the Sierra Leonean government while others point to the international community. Give an example of each.

2) Explain how the diverse factors identified in each part of question 1 are interrelated, and how each contributed to the Sierra Leonean civil war.

3) Explain how the diverse factors identified in each part of question 1 could inform what needs to be addressed in the peace process.

Section Four: Toward Peace and Reconciliation

Most human societies equip individuals with the means for resolving disputes and intervening when informal resolution practices fail. While some societies are oriented more toward revenge and punishment than others, even minimal social stability requires some capacity to forgive rule-violators. Sometimes rituals of forgiveness create a basis for restoring human connection and capacities. But reconciliation practices may suture over deep tensions and differences within group life. These issues are at the heart of the quandaries women describe in this section of *Speaking Out*—quandaries shared by communities recovering from civil conflicts throughout the world. *Speaking Out* is part of a broader program of research on women and war that began with a series of interviews with women in refugee camps in Guinea. These women had fled the fighting in Sierra Leone, often gathering up whatever children were within reach as they fled across the border to seek safety. A tenuous peace accord was in place in August 1999, during the humid month of our visit, and many of the women discussed their uneasiness over the terms of the accord. The Lomé peace agreement provided amnesty for many Revolutionary United Front (RUF) commanders as a condition of their surrender, as well as calling for a process of national reconciliation.

During the interviewing, as women discussed their experiences, some women related stories of youths who had joined the rebels and burned down their own villages. The problem of how to forgive and forget weighed heavily on their minds. Some women stressed the importance of forgetting the past and looking to the future. "We have to put it at our backs," Bondu Mani, with the women's group at Guéckédou refugee camp insisted, "If you dwell on the past, the trauma will never leave you. The way we do this is by engaging in activity together, by working together." Other women stressed remembering as vital to the process of recovery. As Sister Catherine Dauda, Director of the Children's Center of Hope, explained, "We have to understand why this happened to us. If you do not deal with the past, the past will never leave you." In the refugee camps, children and adults came together to create theater and music reenacting and reworking their memories of the war. The refugees also taught each other skills and found creative ways of remembering the positive side of the cultural past.

Women struggled with the question of whom to hold responsible as the primary perpetrators of the war. Was it the young men and boys who joined a violent rebel movement? Are corrupt government officials and local chiefs who made deals with foreign governments and investors while turning their backs on their own people to blame? How is the International Monetary Fund, the institution that forced the government to lay off a third of its public sector workforce just prior to the outbreak of the war implicated? Was it the continuing impact of colonialism, or the international diamond trade and the global economy—systems that extract raw materials from Africa without building the productive capacities of its peoples?

While women differed in where they placed the primary blame, there was considerable agreement that it was difficult to locate a single cause of the conflict. Some of the perpetrators of the war were more easily identified than were others. But social understandings predominated over individualistic ones, as women struggled to find some grounds for hope—a means of bridging the unbearable suffering they and their families had endured. The issue was not whether forgiveness was good or bad, nor was it simply a matter of dispensing forgiveness in some direct proportion to the scale of crimes committed. For many Sierra Leonean women there were two key areas to address in the peace process. First, it was important to recognize the social conditions that led to the war, including those conditions necessary for a lasting peace. Second, it was vital to find means of reintegrating transgressors into their communities and repairing ruptured relationships in communities affected by the war.

Section Four focuses on the varied and creative ways in which Sierra Leoneans are addressing the aftermath of civil war, from dilemmas associated with forgiveness to governmental mechanisms such as the Truth and Reconciliation Commission and the Special Court. Lesson 1, "Retrospective," features an interview with two Sierra Leonean peace activists living in the United States: Jariatu Sesay and Fatima Jarieu Bona. In addressing the question of how to distribute responsibility for the war, these women also explain essential components of the peace process and the relative success of the Truth and Reconciliation Commission and Special Court. Lesson 2, "Stories from Yatta Samah and Corinne Dufka," introduces accounts from two women working in Sierra Leone more directly on these same issues. Lesson 3, "Forgiveness Story," promotes reflection on the process of forgiveness. The activity introduces students to the difficulty of this process by asking them to identify barriers to forgiveness and to explore the conditions necessary for forgiveness to occur. In Lesson 4, "Role Play: Reintegrating Child Soldiers," students watch the third segment of *Diamonds, Guns, and Rice* to better understand dilemmas Sierra Leoneans face in the aftermath of the civil war, particularly in reintegrating former child soldiers. After watching the documentary segment, students participate in an activity designed to help them work through key issues confronting communities in the prospect of reintegrating child ex-combatants into their villages. Lesson 5, "International Tribunal," examines procedures for addressing human rights abuses associated with the Sierra Leonean civil war and debates concerning healing and reparation.

Lesson 1 Retrospective

Time: Approximately 50 minutes

Materials:

Handout: "Jariatu Sesay and Fatima Jarieu Bona: Retrospective"

Procedure:

Distribute "Jariatu Sesay and Fatima Jarieu Bona: Retrospective." Allow students time to read the interview.

Divide the class into small discussion groups (3–4 students). Ask students to discuss the following questions:

What factors does each woman believe must be addressed in the peace process? What would be accomplished by addressing each of these factors?

What strategies does each woman endorse to further the peace process? What factors underlying the war can be addressed through these strategies? Explain.

How do these women evaluate the relative success of the Truth and Reconciliation Commission and the Special Court? How could each organization further the peace process? What do these women find problematic about these organizations in the peace process?

Ask for volunteers from each group to summarize their group's discussion for the rest of the class.

Facilitate a class discussion based on themes in students' responses.

Homework: Ask students to write an essay summarizing what factors Sesay and Bona thought contributed to the war, what each emphasizes as essential for the peace process, and how each evaluates mechanisms instituted by the Sierra Leonean government. Students should also include what they would recommend to further the peace process.

Lesson 2   Stories from Yatta Samah and Corinne Dufka

Time: Approximately 50 minutes

Materials:

> Handouts: "Yatta Samah: The Truth and Reconciliation Commission" and "Corinne Dufka: The Special Court"

Procedure:

> Distribute Yatta Samah: The Truth and Reconciliation Commission" and "Corinne Dufka: The Special Court." Allow students time to read the interviews.

> Divide the class into small discussion groups (3–4 students). Ask students to discuss the following questions:

>> Describe the Truth and Reconciliation Commission and Special Court. What could each contribute to the peace process? Explain how these contributions are complementary or contradictory.

>> Compare Dufka and Samah's perspectives on the Truth and Reconciliation Commission and Special Court. How are they similar and how are they different? What critiques does each woman offer?

>> What explanations do these women offer for youths attacking their own communities? What causes do they emphasize?

>> How do motivations for youths joining rebels in Sierra Leone compare to motivations for youth to join gangs in the U.S.?

> Facilitate a class discussion based on responses from the groups.

Homework: Ask students to write a two-page essay based on the following questions:

> What primary reasons do Dufka and Samah offer in explaining why youth joined the fighting forces in Sierra Leone?

> In discussing the value of the Truth and Reconciliation Commission and the Special Court of Sierra Leone, how do Dufka and Samah agree and how do they disagree?

> Based on the readings, what conclusions would you draw concerning the best mechanisms for achieving reconciliation in Sierra Leone, and what obstacles would need to be addressed?

Lesson 3 Forgiveness Story

Time: Approximately 50 minutes

Note: In most cases, students draw on their own experiences to participate in class discussions. This exercise may elicit emotional responses from some students. Teachers may want to be attuned to those students who have strong personal reactions to the exercise.

Materials:

> Handouts: "Field Research: Interview with Susan Shepler" and "The Role of Interim Care Centers in Reintegration of Child Soldiers" (both used in the Homework).

Procedure:

> Ask students to write a brief response to the questions below. (Allow approximately 20 minutes.) Inform students that after they respond to the questions individually, they will exchange essays and respond to the same questions based on their partner's essay as well as their own.

>> Describe an occasion when someone did something harmful to you, your family, or your community.

>> Did that person do anything to earn forgiveness, such as apologize or make other forms of reparation?

>> To what degree were you able to forgive that person? Totally, partially? Why or why not?

Divide the class into pairs. Ask partners to read each other's essay and briefly discuss together one of the questions below. Students write a one-page response to one of the questions below drawing on their partner's story.

Note: The aim is to develop listening skills and to understand forgiveness from another person's perspective. The questions also may be used as a homework assignment.

> If the transgressor earned forgiveness, what did they say and do?

> If the person was forgiven, how was forgiveness expressed or granted? What are some steps to forgiving?

> If the person was not forgiven, why not? What are some barriers to forgiveness?

> What issues do you think might arise for victims if a person is forgiven too quickly?

Homework: In preparing for the role-play in the next lesson, distribute "Field Research: Interview with Susan Shepler" (See Section One, Lesson 4) and "The Role of Interim Care Centers in Reintegration of Child Soldiers." Based on these handouts, ask students to write a one-page essay. The essay should identify and discuss two potential conflicts for village elders in deciding whether or not to reintegrate former child combatants back into their communities.

Lesson 4 Role Play: Reintegrating Child Soldiers

Time: Approximately two 50-minute class periods

Grief Work

In the process of making the documentary, we met with Sierra Leonean refugees and immigrants to look at whatever photos they could retrieve from relatives abroad. We explained that the aim was to capture the beauty of Sierra Leonean culture as well as the devastation of the war. There were tearful moments as we looked at photos of smartly dressed teenage girls standing arm-in-arm on a green hillside. And we wondered whether these same girls were now dead or alive. Musu Kanu and Karufu Karoma, cousins living in Portland, Oregon who helped with our research, told us about the rural area where the girls lived and how the residents there had been forced to evacuate their villages.

Looking at photos and making selections for the documentary allowed us as outsiders to pay respect to those in our own community who had been affected by the war. For many of the Sierra Leonean women involved in our project, recovering the fragments of history—through stories, photos, and documents—also became part of their own grief work. From a psychological perspective, grief work includes finding means of holding and preserving images of what has been lost, and of finding hope for the future that survives in spite of the loss.

Note: This activity is not a simulation of actual decision-making practices in Sierra Leone, although it does draw on some elements of cultural practices. Instead, it is a tool for generating classroom discussion and for structuring the processes that are carried out more informally in village communities. The role-play is from the perspectives of elders who consider whether two child soldiers—a boy and a girl—should be taken back into the community. Although class time may limit this activity to one of the cases, the use of both allows the teacher to draw out and explore gender issues in community responses to returning child soldiers.

Day 1: Perspectives

Materials:

> Documentary: Part III, "Peace," from *Diamonds, Guns, and Rice* (Cue time: 31:55; Running time: 13:05) (Note: If students have not seen the Introduction, Part I, and Part II, teachers may want to show the documentary from the beginning.)

> Handouts: "Discussing the Reintegration of Child Soldiers" and "Decision Process Guidelines"

Procedure:

> Distribute "Discussing the Reintegration of Child Soldiers." Ask students to take notes on the questions listed while watching the documentary. Show Part III, "Peace," from *Diamonds, Guns, and Rice*. Advise students that they will use their notes to complete a homework assignment.

> Divide the class into small groups (3–4 students). Ask groups to discuss each question on "Discussing the Reintegration of Child Soldiers." Students should use this time to develop their individual responses.

> Facilitate a class discussion by asking a volunteer from each group to report the group's responses to each question. Students should use this opportunity to elaborate on their answers.

> Distribute "Decision Process Guidelines" and ask students to read the handout.

> Review the handout with the students. Ask students to note their responses to the first three steps while going over the handout in class. Students will further develop those responses in the homework assignment.

Homework: Ask students to further elaborate their responses to the first three steps on the handout "Decision Process Guidelines" and write a one-page response to step four (Note: Step four makes reference to Interim Care Centers, which are described in the handout "The Role of Interim Care Centers in Reintegration of Child Soldiers" distributed in Lesson 3 of this Section). Essays should draw on students' own ideas, their responses to the first three steps of the handout, and their responses to questions posed in the handout "Discussing the Reintegration of Child Soldiers."

Day 2: Role Play

Materials:

Handouts: "Decision Process Guidelines" (from Day 1), "Child Soldier A: Fatou Kamera," "Child Soldier B: Abbas Fofanah," "Village Elder 1: Alimani Mansaray," "Village Elder 2: Tichaona Dumbaya," and "Village Elder 3: Amara Fomba."

Procedure:

In this lesson students explore the question, "Under what conditions should former child soldiers be reintegrated into their communities?" Students are divided into two Village Councils, each of which deliberates on the case of a different child soldier.

Each Village Council is divided into three groups (for a total of six groups), each of which is assigned the perspective of one of three Elders on the Village Council (Village Elder 1, Village Elder 2, and Village Elder 3). The first Village Council (groups 1 through 3) considers the case of "Child Soldier A: Fatou Kamera." The second Village Council (groups 4 through 6) considers the case of "Child Soldier B: Abbas Fofanah." In their groups, students read narratives illustrating the perspective of their assigned Elder and describing the case of one of two child soldiers.

Groups then answer the questions on "Decision Process Guidelines." Once groups decide on a course of action, each group (representing an Elder on the Village Council) presents recommendations to an audience. The two separate Village Councils deliberating on different child soldier cases take place sequentially such that Village Council I acts as an audience for Village Council II and vice-versa.

First divide students into two Village Councils. Next divide each Council into three groups, each of which represents the perspective of a different Elder (for a total of six groups)

Distribute "Decision Process Guidelines" if students do not have the handout from Day 1.

Distribute the other handouts as follows:

Village Council I: Deciding on Child Soldier A: Fatou Kamera

Group 1: "Village Elder 1: Alimani Mansaray" and "Child Soldier A: Fatou Kamera"

Group 2: "Village Elder 2: Tichaona Dumbaya" and "Child Soldier A: Fatou Kamera"

Group 3: "Village Elder 3: Amara Fomba" and "Child Soldier A: Fatou Kamera"

Village Council II: Deciding on Child Soldier B: Abbas Fofanah

> Group 4: "Village Elder 1: Alimani Mansaray" and "Child Soldier B: Abbas Fofanah"
>
> Group 5: "Village Elder 2: Tichaona Dumbaya" and "Child Soldier B: Abbas Fofanah"
>
> Group 6: "Village Elder 3: Amara Fomba" and "Child Soldier B: Abbas Fofanah"

Ask groups to read their respective Elder and child soldier handouts. Groups should then use the "Decision Process Guidelines" to develop a course of action regarding reintegrating the former child soldier from the perspective of their assigned Elder. (Allow approximately 20 minutes.) Inform students that each Elder will have three minutes to present their position during their council meeting.

When groups finish, ask Village Council I (groups 1 through 3) to sit on one side of the room and ask Village Council II (groups 4 through 6) to sit on the opposite side. Explain that Village Council II acts as an audience while Elders from Village Council I present their courses of action, and Village Council I is an audience for Elders from Village Council II during their presentations.

Distribute the child soldier case discussed by the Council to the audience prior to the presentation, i.e., distribute "Child Soldier A: Fatou Kamera" to Village Council I, and "Child Soldier B: Abbas Fofanah" to Village Council II. Allow each Council approximately 20 minutes to read the case.

Ask a volunteer from each group to represent the Elder and summarize their course of action to the audience. Explain that volunteers from each group are not the Elder's sole representative, and invite all students assigned that particular perspective to contribute to the presentation. Ask Elders from Village Council I to present, starting with Village Elder 1, then 2, and ending with 3. Next ask Village Elder Council II to present, starting with Village Elder 3, then 1, and ending with 2.

Homework: Ask students to write a one-page essay summarizing their respective child soldier's case, the position of their elder, and any conclusions they drew from the role-play. Students should refer to the "Decision Process Guidelines" to discuss courses of action the community might pursue in implementing different decisions.

Lesson 5   International Tribunal

Time: Approximately two 50-minute class periods

The Khulumani Lawsuit Corporate Accountability for Apartheid

The Khulumani Support Group is a human rights organization that grew out of the anti-apartheid struggle and the reconciliation process. In November 2002 the group filed a lawsuit in New York against a number of foreign corporations that benefited from the apartheid system in South Africa. The Khulumani lawsuit seeks to engage corporations in a dialogue about what they might contribute towards repairing the damage done to individuals and communities in South Africa.

The suit used the Alien Tort Claims Act 1789—controversial legislation allowing companies to be sued in American courts for human rights violations committed anywhere that companies operate. Khulumani's lawsuit seeks to hold 23 multinational corporations accountable for their role in contributing to an environment in which gross violations of human rights were made possible. The Khulumani suit extends the legal struggle to include the practices of governments and foreign corporations and provides redress for violations of universally recognized human rights standards.

Day 1: Introducing Players on the International Tribunal

Materials:

Handouts: "Prosecuting De Beers," "Prosecuting Small Arms Manufacturers," "Defending De Beers," "Defending Small Arms Dealers," "Judging the International Tribunal," "Blood Diamonds," and "Small Arms: The Real Weapons of Mass Destruction?" (See Section Three, Lesson 4)

Procedure:

Explain to students that they will be dramatizing an International Tribunal during the next two class meetings. On the first day the groups prepare their roles and on the second day they create the role-play.

Write all five groups involved in the role play on the board: De Beers Corporation Prosecutors, Small Arms Manufacturers Prosecutors, De Beers Corporation Defense Attorneys, Small Arms Manufacturers Defense Attorneys, and Judges.

Select four to six students to act as Judges on the International Tribunal. Judges will listen to arguments, ask questions of the Defense Attorneys and the Prosecution, and make decisions concerning guilt and rulings. Distribute "Judging the International Tribunal," "Blood Diamonds" and "Small Arms: The Real Weapons of Mass Destruction?" to the Judges.

Divide the remaining students into two groups. Designate one group as Prosecutors and the other as Defense Attorneys. Prosecutors prepare arguments, recommend rulings, and respond to questions from the Judges. Defense Attorneys prepare arguments and respond to questions from the Judges.

Divide the group of Prosecutors into two groups: De Beers Corporation Prosecutors and Small Arms Manufacturers Prosecutors. Distribute "Prosecuting De Beers" and "Blood Diamonds" to the De Beers Corporation Prosecutors. Distribute "Prosecuting Small Arms Dealers" and "Small Arms: The Real Weapons of Mass Destruction?" to the Small Arms Manufacturers Prosecutors.

Divide the group of Defense Attorneys into two groups: Defense Attorneys for the De Beers Corporation and Defense Attorneys for the Small Arms Manufacturers. The two defending parties can choose to work together or argue separately to displace blame onto the other.

Distribute "Defending De Beers" and "Blood Diamonds" to the De Beers Corporation Defense Attorneys. Distribute "Defending Small Arms Manufacturers" and "Small Arms: The Real Weapons of Mass Destruction?" to the Small Arms Manufacturers Defense Attorneys.

Ask students to read all their handouts and to work with their groups to complete the assignment for their respective role.

Source:

Hamber, B. (2004). Amicus Brief in Support of Khulumani's Lawsuit. Retrieved July 2005 from Brandon Hamber's Web site: http://www.brandonhamber.com/documents/legalaction-press3.htm

Day 2: Role Play

Materials:

> Name tags

Procedure:

> Use name tags to identify which role each student is playing. Ask students to sit in a circle. Make sure that each group sits together.

> Ask for a volunteer from each group of Defense Attorneys and Prosecutors to present their case before the Judges. While this student is the spokesperson, all students are encouraged to contribute to the debate.

> Judges will call each case one at a time. First, Judges will ask the De Beers Prosecutors to read the charges against the De Beers Corporation. Second, the De Beers Defense Attorneys will defend against those charges. Third, Judges may ask the De Beers Prosecutors and Defense Attorneys questions. Last, Prosecutors may recommend possible punishments. The Small Arms Manufacturers will present their case next. First, Judges will ask the Small Arms Manufacturers Prosecutors to read the charges against the Small Arms Manufacturers. Second, the Small Arms Manufacturers Defense Attorneys will defend against those charges. Third, Judges may ask the Small Arms Manufacturers Prosecutors and Defense Attorneys questions. Last, Prosecutors may recommend possible punishments. After hearing both cases, Judges will consider all recommendations and make decisions as to degrees of innocence, guilt, or responsibility.

> Ask students to write an essay addressing the following questions:

>> What was the outcome of the role-play in each case? Was the Judges' decision fair? Why or why not?

>> What were the most important points made in the role-play? Did any of the arguments surprise you?

>> Did your perception of who is to blame for the civil war change over the course of the activity? How?

Jariatu Sesay and Fatima Jarieu Bona: Retrospective

Jariatu Sesay grew up in Freetown, Sierra Leone. As the eldest daughter in a large family, from an early age, she helped to put food on the table. Sesay arrived in the United States as a refugee in the early 1990s, where she became a mobilizing voice for peace, human rights, and women's empowerment. During her country's terrible civil war she carried out this political work while putting her university education on hold. She produced videos and radio interviews calling for the international community to "open the blinds" and see what was happening in Sierra Leone. She was a founding member of the Sierra Leone Women's Movement for Peace, New Jersey branch in the United States. As a member of the African community in New Jersey, Sesay meets with other U.S.-based survivors of the war to help these families learn the skills they need to go from crisis to recovery. She also is pursuing a Masters in Conflict Analysis and Resolution, which she plans to use to prevent future violence in the world.

Fatima Jarieu Bona was born in Freetown, Sierra Leone, in 1954. She attended the Freetown Secondary School for Girls and the Saint Helena School. After immigrating to the United States in 1980, Bona received her B.A. in Sociology from Edison College in Trenton, New Jersey. She worked for a number of charity organizations and served as the customer coordinator for Associated Press. A dedicated wife, mother, and community peace activist, she is currently Chairperson for the Sierra Leonean Women's Movement for Peace, Member of the African Women's Charity Organization and Social Secretary for the Sierra Leone American National Association. Bona's greatest aspiration has been to help people.

Haaken: When I interviewed you for our documentary in 1999, both of you emphasized the importance of economic factors, such as the international diamond trade and arms dealing, in understanding causes of the civil war. Now that the country is engaged in rebuilding and reconciliation, how do these same economic factors—both national and international—play a role?

Sesay: Now that we have cessation of hostilities, the dust has settled down for us to take a closer look at our civil war. There were many factors, other than economic reasons, igniting and encouraging our conflict. Therefore, we will have to explore different avenues to pursue peace and resolve our conflict. Cessation of hostilities does not signify the end to our war, nor does the influx of foreign aid ease our economic burden.

It is sad to say that we are still considered one of the poorest countries in the world, even though we have diamonds, gold, bauxite, and a very fertile land. We are still going through rampant inflation, currency devaluation, budget deficits, corruption, and declining exports—which is creating fuel, power, and food shortages as I respond to this interview. Youth unemployment is still growing, as well as student radicalism. This is exactly what led to our civil war, and there is no effort from the current government to change the situation. If nothing is done soon, we may face a second conflict, which will be worse than the one we just had.

Bona: With economic stability, comes stable community. Now that the guns are silent, the focus should be on the economic development of the country. On the local level the government should try very hard for the eradication of corruption, which seems to be ingrained in the society. In turn our government would earn the respect and trust of international bodies, which will lead to their participation in our economic development. Without these efforts, the process of attaining total peace will be easier for violators to undermine.

Haaken: Jariatu and Fatima, you also have worked together for many years to bring women's voices into discussions about war and reconciliation. The Sierra Leone Women's Movement for Peace was a vital forum for Sierra Leonean women in exile who needed to speak out. How do you see the situation of women in Sierra Leone today, after the truth and reconciliation process?

Sesay: The conflict in Sierra Leone highlights the unique role of women during and after our conflict. Women served as sex slaves and human shields for the Revolutionary United Front (RUF) fighters, and those women who were attached to RUF fighters also protected some of the girls who were abducted into the fighting forces.

In a country like Sierra Leone where there is still a conflict brewing, women's peace-building strategies at both local and international levels will continue to play a key role in the future peace and security of Sierra Leone. It was the women who were willing to welcome the child soldiers into their midst in spite of the havoc these kids had wreaked on them. One of the advantages we have as women in Sierra Leone today is the influx of nongovernmental organizations (NGOs), such as the Marie Stopes Society, that cater to the needs of women. We have always been the backbone of the country's economy. But if you go to Sierra Leone today, there is a "role reversal syndrome" affecting a majority of our households. The majority of women are the breadwinner as well as the head of the household today.

Bona: It is obvious that during the conflict in Sierra Leone, women suffered the brunt of it all. They endured the deaths of their children, husbands, and other loved ones, and were victims of rape and other atrocities. Left to pick up the pieces despite their own sufferings, women were forced to take charge and accept responsibilities beyond their wildest expectations. They have now become a force to reckon with. Women's organizations like the Women's Movement for Peace, NGOs, and other women's groups played important roles in bringing peace to Sierra Leone and are still fighting for peace, especially in addressing health care and economic opportunities for women and youth. We have women in leading roles today in Sierra Leone, but we could increase the number both locally and internationally.

Haaken: Can you say something about your families in Sierra Leone and how they have been changed by the war?

Sesay: I lost my father and several uncles during the war. Our family will never be the same again, but, like everybody else in the country, we have no choice but to move on.

On the other hand, it has been an economic burden on my sister and I to send money to our family back home. I had to put my education on hold for a while to make sure they were taken care of during the war. Now that I have resumed pursuing my education, it is still a burden on both of us because there is change in our economy. I will say that it's getting worse by the minute.

Bona: As for my family it was a wake-up call. There is more love and closeness now than ever. Because of the deaths and destruction of properties that we endured, we seem to appreciate each other more and regard this as a second chance given by God. Economically it is not easy, especially for someone like me who came from a very large family. In my family, if you are blessed with a little more than the next person, it is your responsibility to help.

Haaken: In your views, what are the key factors in the peace process? Have the Truth and Reconciliation Commission (TRC) and the Special Court been successful in your view?

Sesay: We have to be willing to take a good look at ourselves and accept criticism on the mistakes we have made since we gained independence. Our country is still descending into the abyss, and we may not be able to dig ourselves out of it if we don't speak up now. The guns have been silenced, this is the time for us to raise our voices and speak up about the ills of society if we want the peace process to continue. We should not wait for some hoodlums to raise their guns against us.

The Lomé Accord of July 7, 1999, provides for the establishment of a TRC to address impunity, break the cycle of violence, provide a forum for both the victims and perpetrators of human rights violations to tell their story, and get a clear picture of the past in order to facilitate genuine healing and reconciliation. Then, at the request of the government of Sierra Leone, the United Nations proposed establishing an international court for prosecution of those responsible for the commission of atrocities during the war. UN Security Council Resolution 1315, adopted on August 14, 2000, calls for a Special Court to prosecute those who bear the greatest responsibility for crimes against humanity, war crimes, and other serious violations of international humani-

tarian law. For the most part these were high commanders in the RUF.

In my opinion, the government and United Nations should have waited until after the TRC had completed its work before proposing the Special Court; that way we would have been able to gather enough evidence to prosecute those who bear the greatest responsibility for these crimes. In the Lomé Accord, we gave the rebels blanket amnesty because we were tired of the war, and we wanted it to end. We then encouraged them to come forward and tell the whole truth and nothing but the truth so that we will be able to move forward. The government did not even wait for the ink to dry on the peace accord when they announced that there would also be a Special Court running simultaneously.

Haaken: Many critics of Truth and Reconciliation Commissions around the world emphasize the importance of the timing of these processes. There are also concerns about whether it is helpful to criminalize participants who cannot be easily classified as either victims or perpetrators.

Sesay: In my view, it was a disaster running the TRC and Special Court simultaneously. During the TRC, most the perpetrators were afraid to tell the truth because they did not want to be seen as "those persons who bear the greatest responsibility for the civil war." If nothing had been mentioned about the Special Court, we would have been able to gather enough information to go after those we think bear the greatest guilt in our war, and go after them with an iron fist.

Bona: Let me first of all start by saying that I believe people should pay for the crimes they committed, especially the vicious ones committed by some of these people. The rapes, opening the stomach of pregnant women, maiming, killing, the list goes on and on. The TRC and the Special Court were formed by the Sierra Leone government and the United Nations to prosecute these crimes and other serious violations against humanity. At this point I'm not sure if I'm in the position to profess success, but only to state that they are trying to do the job bestowed upon them.

Sesay: Our war was a strange war, and so is the peace process. The government was quick to say, "we want you to speak the truth, but after that we are also going to come after those who committed the worst crimes." In my opinion, it's a smart way to cover their tracks by telling the rebels to be careful about what they tell the TRC, because the amnesty that was given to them will not apply if they say too much. We will never know who were the real perpetrators in our war, and that's going to affect our peace process.

Yatta Samah: The Truth and Reconciliation Commission

Yatta Samah is of the Mende tribe. She was born in Kenema town in the district of Kenema, located in the eastern region where the civil war initially broke out. She received a teacher's certificate from Freetown Teachers College, and when the war started in 1991, Samah decided to concentrate her energy on educating and mobilizing women. She taught women about their rights, how they could help maintain peace, and how to leave behind the atrocities of the war and focus on positive means of healing. Samah won the Women's Creativity in Rural Life gold medal laureate award in 2000 from the Women's World Summit Foundation in Geneva, Switzerland for working with rural women. In 2004, her work was recognized by FAO in Rome as the best women's farming organization in Sierra Leone. As a community activist Samah organized a women's farming collective that led to the Moawoma Rural Women's Development Association (MORWO-DAS). Describing herself as an ecofeminist, Samah works across different regions in Sierra Leone, helping the area recover from the devastation suffered on all levels during the civil war. Under Samah's leadership, the Moawama organization continues to grow as a grassroots nongovernmental organization (NGO) for rural women's empowerment.

In an interview focused on women, economics, and the peace process, Jan Haaken asks Yatta Samah about her own experience in organizing a rural women's farming cooperative.

Haaken: Your approach to the peace process focuses on building new economic opportunities for youth, as well as giving testimony to what people experienced during the war. Could you describe your rural organizing project and how this work is related to the peace process?

Samah: The Moawoma Rural Women's Development Association (MORWODAS) is an indigenous non-governmental organization that first started as a community-based organization in April 1995, during the height of the civil war. While interviewing women in Kenema I found that most of them were the breadwinners in their homes. The men were staying inside because they were afraid of being accused of collaborating with the enemy by the various warring factions. I initiated the idea of cooperating across differing ethnic groups, as women, to stabilize our situations for survival and economic empowerment. This effort has grown to become a large women's cooperative organization that operates not only in Kenema but also in other districts. We have established the Association based on the desire for a program that would draw urgently needed attention to the plight of rural women, who produce about 60–80 percent of foods consumed in Sierra Leone. Its programs include agricultural and other sustainable income-generating

activities, skill training, promotion of health and sanitation, and education on the civic rights of women and children. To build a strong foundation MORWODAS has made long-term investments in food production, training staff, and constructing buildings.

MORWODAS is the first and the only Association that has won two Gold Medals: the first in 2000 from the Women's World Summit Foundation and the second from the Food and Agricultural Organization in 2002. The Association is different from other economic development projects in that it is the first owned and managed solely by women. The women come from five adjacent chiefdoms (counties): Dama, Koya, Gaura, Tunkia, and Nomo. Located behind the Moa River in the Kenema District of Eastern Sierra Leone, these five chiefdoms are referred to as the Moawoma Community.

Central to the MORWODAS mission is serving and empowering women, especially those living in the Moawoma Community. Since its conception, membership in the organization has soared to over 10,000. The Association brings women together through their traditional work as farmers, as well as in new ways across ethnic lines, for example, in building on common spiritual principles across Christianity, Islam, and Animism and in finding how respect for women, working for peace, and a healthy environment are all connected. MORWODAS helps rural women rehabilitate themselves, alleviate their poverty, and effectively integrate into society in the spirit of mutual aid and self-development.

Haaken: In many countries, women are either excluded from or reluctant to participate in Truth and Reconciliation Commissions (TRCs). What was this process like for the women in Sierra Leone?

Samah: In Sierra Leone's Truth and Reconciliation program, there was no discrimination on a gender basis. All participated freely and equally. Women who had been sexually abused gave testimonies on camera. They vented their experiences to release the stress in them. After their testimonies, they were able to overcome their trauma. The TRC also gave recognition to the treatment of women, and how the poor status of women in society made women victims to terrible human rights abuses.

Haaken: Some feel that the TRC is a better procedure and some feel the Special Court is better in addressing the injustices of the war. What is your view of these two procedures?

Samah: If we are able to forget the past, we will be in a position to start rebuilding our battered lives. The TRC told us that we have to move forward and to "forgive and forget," but the Special Court just incarcerates people. Although it is important to prosecute the leaders involved in human rights violations, we have not seen benefit yet from the Special Court. The TRC opened the wounds of the war by getting testimony, but the TRC also encouraged dialogue and programs for healing. The Special Court opens old wounds and leaves them open. For example, if I was raped and tell my story or if I say what happened to my sister and they do nothing about it, I am just re-traumatized. That is what has happened with the Special Court. So it has not so far been a good thing for us.

Haaken: Whether people are able to forgive depends on how they understand why the rebels committed the atrocities. It has been difficult for many people outside the country to understand why these young people often came back to their own villages to attack their own communities, and sometimes their own families. How do you understand that?

Samah: The war was basically a youth war. More youths participated than any other age group. Most fighters were below the age of twenty. The youths often came back to burn down houses in their own villages, sometimes attacking their families, because they had been treated very badly and abused by their elders. Sometimes the young men fall in love with the wives of the elders and have no resources to marry, so they resent the older men. These boys would face fines imposed by the elder men in their villages, maybe for having relationships with women who were in forced marriages. So the girls, too, went to the bush and took up arms because they were angry over their bad treatment. Many of these girls do not want to go back now to their villages because they were forced into marriages, denied an education, and treated very badly.

Corinne Dufka: The Special Court of Sierra Leone

Corinne Dufka is an award-winning photojournalist who has documented conflicts from Central America to the Balkans and Africa. In late 2003, Dufka received a "genius" award from the MacArthur Foundation in recognition of her work documenting and investigating war crimes in Sierra Leone. Dufka first came to Sierra Leone in April 1999, where she lived and worked for about five years. At that time she served as the West Africa team leader for Human Rights Watch, setting up their office in Freetown to oversee their work in Liberia and Sierra Leone. From October 2002 through October 2003, Dufka was an investigator for the Special Court of Sierra Leone. She carried out investigations of human rights abuses based on accounts from first-hand witnesses to elevate awareness of the gravity of the human rights violations on all sides in the Sierra Leonean civil war. As an investigator, she advocated for victims, produced a number of reports, and continuously briefed nongovernmental organizations (NGOs) and policy makers.

Haaken: One of the questions that comes up a lot in showing our documentary and putting the civil war in a context is why these youths sometimes attacked their own families and villages. Usually you think of war—even civil war—as organized around in-group / out-group relations. Violence is more apt to be carried out against groups defined as the "other." How did you come to understand violence committed by youth against their own communities?

Dufka: That was always of interest to us as well. With any war, there is an element of dehumanization that goes on. In many conflicts, it's on the basis of their religion or ethnicity. But it's hard to say. Part of it is that there was a process of turning normal kids into very violent creatures where their human capacities were undermined with use of drugs. Rebels also created a very close-knit culture that did create protective bonds in the midst of the chaos overwhelming the country.

Haaken: Several women we interviewed in refugee camps talked about older grievances within families, among sons, with young sons coming back and having fewer opportunities in life. Did you have any of those stories—where local grievances get pulled into a civil war?

Dufka: Oh yes, many of the rebels had been expelled from their communities because the could not pay the fines imposed by the local authorities or elders. These kids had been fined so much money that when they could not pay the fines, they had been expelled from their communities and became social outcasts. And when they came back with the rebels, they attacked their own communities. I found that this was quite common.

Haaken: Some women we spoke with in Guéckédou mentioned that problem—that the youth had been treated harshly by the elders.

Dufka: Yes, and there was a kind of resentment. In Sierra Leone, you have such a dichotomy, where on the one hand you have a very conservative culture where people are very reluctant to confront elders, or confront any symbol of authority. Yet on the other hand, once the elements of social control are taken off, they go all out. They will go all out to punish those whom they blame to have failed and exploited them. That is why you have these local political party members who were so brutally targeted, particularly during the early years of the conflict. And yet it is a very conservative society, much more than in Liberia.

Haaken: In any society, authority has to have material resources to maintain control over youth. Once the authority breaks down, and the elders can only crack down on youth and have very little else to give, you have a basis for a youth rebellion.

Dufka: The Sierra Leonean war was in large part the result of people being betrayed by the people who were supposed to protect them—the army, the police, politicians. These people were seen as basically parasites, so there was a tremendous amount of resentment built up in people.

Haaken: There are different forms of youth rebellion, and some forms of rebellion are quite constructive. Do you think the Revolutionary United Front (RUF) began with legitimate grievances?

Dufka: Yes, they did begin with genuine grievances, and if they had respected human rights, they would have really swept the country like wildfire. During the first attack in 1991, however, there were violations against civilians. What's interesting about it is that in the beginning, most of the rebels who attacked the villages were Liberians. So it didn't come from this wellspring of youth fomenting rebellion. It was Liberians who provoked this, and the primary method of recruitment throughout the war was forced abduction. So it became a revolution by default. I see that as a risk in what is happening now. They know about revolution because they have had one. They now know that that is on the menu of options—having an armed uprising.

Haaken: Is that a completely corrupting lesson or is there potential for multiple outcomes, in tasting the bitter fruit of knowing you can create an uprising?

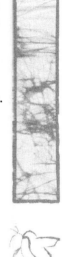

Dufka: Human Rights Watch does not take a position on armed revolution because there are good ones and bad ones. Look at our own American Revolution and the French Revolution, although the French whacked a lot of heads in that one. What we say is that if there is going to be a revolution, warring parties need to abide by human rights. Sometimes the government is so bad, and when they have used other means and methods available within civil society, then some people might come to the conclusion that that is the only way to change things.

Haaken: Is part of what they have learned, that you can win things this way?

Dufka: Unfortunately, one of the lessons learned by the leaders of the revolution, the RUF, is that not only did they get away with the atrocities they committed, but they were rewarded for them. That is a very dangerous lesson. That's why we come out very strongly against any kind of amnesty for the leaders.

Haaken: Isn't it a kind of gang psychology, with some of the factors you would find in these desperate situations of youth the same as you would find in the US?

Dufka: Yes, it's a gang psychology in a sense. Sierra Leoneans also are very traumatized by hunger. It is amazing how important food is and how difficult it is to satisfy very basic needs. People have described their attachment to the rebels because they could eat well; youth saying they got to eat meat every day. Just as an example, there was a guy whose wife was an abductee, and I commented that "you must have been very upset to see your wife abducted by these rebels." He said, "but the rebels had rice."

Haaken: That's one reason we called this documentary *Diamonds, Guns, and Rice*. The rice holds tremendous symbolic power, representing what is most sustaining in life, as well as the basic conditions of survival.

Dufka: These people had been subjected to tremendous abuse and exploitation by their authority figures, so the rebels took advantage of that. Even the situation of women abducted into sexual service grew out of older problems with male authority. The relationship between a traditional wife and the bush wife is not so different—both are subject to domination by their husbands.

Haaken: We have been trying to be very careful to put all of this in a context. Yet I have been criticized for putting too much emphasis on the outside players. We feel that it is up to Sierra Leoneans to confront their own corrupt leaders, but our

responsibility as Westerners and outsiders is to address how our own leaders are implicated in these conflicts in Africa. How would you distribute moral responsibility for the war?

Dufka: I think it lies pretty squarely on Sierra Leonean political leaders; they made decisions every single day. Of course it did not help that the US and Britain were turning a blind eye to it.

Haaken: That leaves open the question of how these elites were able to operate and how much they depended on the foreign powers and diamond interests to exploit their own people.

Dufka: So certainly foreign powers benefit. The diamond companies can get a higher percent of profits if they are not taxed, or are given a certain number of government contracts.

Haaken: You have focused some on the diamond industry. How much responsibility would you lay at the feet of De Beers? They removed themselves in the 1980s from direct involvement in Sierra Leone, but they continue to control much of the world's diamond reserves.

Dufka: It's not just the diamonds or the amount of diamonds, but how the diamond resources are managed. The country's political leaders have been utterly irresponsible in how they have managed that industry. There is this campaign for Good Governance, however, and women have been very involved in challenging corruption.

Haaken: Now that there have been some procedures in place to address this corruption, how would you evaluate their success? And what do you see as the difference between the Special Court and the Truth and Reconciliation Commission (TRC)? Some question whether the Special Court is the best use of resources—that it prosecutes very few people and brings in lawyers and experts from outside the country.

Dufka: They are very different, of course. Between the two of them, the TRC of course was created to create an impartial, permanent record of the conflict. For them to have done their job is to expose what gave rise to the war and of course some of the violations as well. People generally knew about these violations, but the ones they didn't know about were the ones by the government forces. So it was common knowledge that there was civilian involvement. The TRC exposes these people but it doesn't hold them accountable—it doesn't deal with impunity. But I think it's good because their recommendations are very strong, very far-reaching. And civil society needs to organize itself around implementing those recommendations. Special

Court will be a success not because it's going to presumably convict these 9 or 12 people. No, it will be a success if it rejuvenates Sierra Leoneans' understanding of what justice is in the first place, because they don't get what a properly functioning court and justice system is—because they haven't had one. That is the beauty of it. They need to take these proceedings out to the community, which they are doing in an edited video format. Their plan is to video and edit an hour summary every week, to show how justice operates. It confronts the notion that you do not have the right to confront the big men. That in and of itself is very empowering. Hinga Normon was indicted as head of the Interior Ministry, and this was very powerful, to see that he could be brought to justice.

Haaken: From your perspective, are everyday citizens actively involved in the Special Court process?

Dufka: There are a lot of Sierra Leoneans working in the special court. Part of the Special Court is what they call "legacy"—creating the physical premises of the special court, an actual courtroom in Freetown, which will turn into the Supreme Court. But more important has been the involvement of Sierra Leonean prosecutorial and defense lawyers, investigators and judges. I would say that half of the staff involved in the Special Court are Sierra Leonean professionals.

Haaken: What about the role of women in these proceedings?

Dufka: There are lots of women involved—as police officers, prosecution lawyers, clerical staff and junior professionals.

Haaken: How are they trained to participate in the Court?

Dufka: Many did not have to be trained. There are top-notch lawyers there, as good or better than what you would find here. They did receive some special training, specifically in gender training.

Haaken: What was the extent of the gender sensitivity training? Perhaps you could give an example of what would be included.

Dufka: First, it is getting women to do it, explaining why the questions have to be asked, trying to be sensitive to the difficulty for women in responding to such detailed questions about sexual violations. But this was a unique aspect of the Special Court in Sierra Leone—that it was a central part of the prosecutions and that investigating sexual crimes was built into every one of the indictments.

Haaken: At the community level, how do people participate?

Dufka: From the very beginning, the prosecutors went out into the country to get people on board, where they asked people questions about justice or the lack thereof in Sierra Leone.

Haaken: The TRC included a special report for children. As a psychologist, I am very interested in the problem of how to explain the horror of war to children while also conveying that there are more good people in the world than bad people. But these are children who have lost many of the protective illusions children are granted in other parts of the world.

Dufka: I have written how for many young people in Africa, including Sierra Leone, war is the only work they have. They are mercenaries—not by choice but by necessity. They don't have any other choice but to go with what they know. The government has a responsibility to provide them another way of life. They should have a means of making a living through other means than warfare.

Haaken: In your writing, you also have addressed the emotional costs for you in this type of work. Do you find that there was some risk of becoming cynical, or feeling hopeless? In my own work, it's important to connect with the capacities of people to continue to be creative, and to connect with the positive side of the human experience, even under such destructive circumstances, without turning away from the gravity of the situation. You write about situations where people are being helpful to one another, even under such extraordinary conditions.

Dufka: Yes, that's very important. Forming friendships is important, but bridging cultural differences can be very difficult. Take money, for example. There are very different ideas about asking friends for money in Sierra Leone than in the United States. If people do not use their contacts with outsiders to get resources and money, they are seen by their families and communities as, in a sense, failing in their obligations. So this can be very awkward, and it is hard to separate feeling used from being aware of the desperate situation people are in, and different systems of patronage that have developed over time.

Haaken: Of course there are quiet forms of suffering, daily deaths from disease and starvation, which are less apt to mobilize the international community.

Dufka: War is absolutely tragic and horrible, and people can do something about it, but they need to be educated as well—they need to understand what those images mean, and how to prevent such suffering.

The Role of Interim Care Centers in Reintegration of Child Soldiers

Seiza de Tarr and Jan Haaken

Rebel commanders signed a peace accord in 1999 and secured positions in the new government, encouraging Sierra Leonean rebels on the ground to hand over their weapons to the government in the process of demobilization. Many former child soldiers and youths who were involved in the war returned to their villages, while still others sought a new life in the cities. Whether in the relative anonymity of the city or the familiarity of a rural village, former child soldiers encountered obstacles in reintegrating into society. Just as youths found their way into various rebel groups in a variety of ways, through abduction, through seeking protection, or by choosing to join, they also pursued a range of paths in adapting to the post-conflict situation.

Interim Care Centers (ICCs) were set up by nongovernmental organizations (NGOs) and Sierra Leonean governmental organizations (SLANGOs) in post-war Sierra Leone to help former child combatants reintegrate into society. As part of a formal reintegration process, ICCs provide psychological counseling, education, skills training, and help children locate their families with the primary goal of reintegrating them back into their communities. Some youths, however, find a new life with organizations or families in another town. NGOs offer benefits such as clothes and educational and vocational materials to the children completing their programs. However, ICCs are predominantly designed for and used by former male child soldiers. Although roughly an equal number of boys and girls joined or were abducted by the Revolutionary United Front (RUF), only 5 percent of children in the formal programs are girls. The programs require that former soldiers pass tests for entry based on combat roles more apt to be carried out by males than females, such as disassembling an AK-47.

Returning girl soldiers follow a different post-war integration path than their male counterparts and have different needs. Many return directly to their villages, a process known as spontaneous integration. Children who return via the ICCs are eligible for benefits, such as job training and stipends, but those who do not go through a formal demobilization program are not. Therefore, girls are less likely than boys to receive help in the reintegration process. In a country of scarce resources, female ex-combatants have less access to support in terms of education, medical care, and resources such as school supplies and clothing.

There are some notable exceptions, however. The Forum for African Women Educationalists (FAWE) provides education programs for returning girl soldiers. The International Rescue Committee has also established programs that specifically address the needs of former female combatants, some of who either choose not to return to their communities or are rejected. For these girls, prostitution becomes means of survival. NGOs in Freetown are attempting to reach out to girl prostitutes by providing AIDS education and condoms. The Conforti Center in east Freetown provides protection, education, and vocational skills to young mothers who want to return to their communities. They help in local mediation in such cases as when a female ex-combatant brings a baby home to face rejection by her family, or experiences the stigma of rape in her community. However, these programs are able to serve only a fraction of the girls that could use them.

In the ICCs, the children learn how to present their stories—to create what Susan Shepler terms "discourses of abdicated responsibility." The children learn how to tell the story of their participation in rebel activity, and communities are "sensitized" to be aware of the tendency to blame the youth for their destructive behavior. This does not always lead to reintegration, however. Shepler explains that youths who had some motivation for joining—whether angry with their elders or acting on some grievance—are less accepted than were those who claimed that someone forced them to join the fighting forces.

In the book, *Where Are the Girls?*, researchers Susan McKay and Dyan Mazurana note that youths who were away for longer periods of time, particularly girls, were less

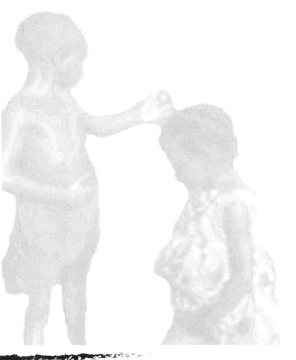

readily accepted back into their communities. The villagers voiced concern that the girls had been "ruined" by their experiences. Shepler explains, "In many cases it is easier for a boy to be accepted after amputating the hands of villagers, than it is for a girl to be accepted after being the victim of rape." Children abducted at the beginning of the war were gone for up to eight years. Many had few memories of their family and villages. Children abducted near the end of the war and gone less than a year, however, had a much easier time reintegrating into their villages.

The road back to rural villages need not mean a return to traditional ways, however. Yattah, and Moawoma Rural Women's Development Association (MORWODAS), offers refuge to girl ex-combatants, creating alternatives between the harsh choice of either returning to restrictive village life or finding their way in a war-torn city. Yattah Samah, one of the organizers of MORWODAS, describes the importance of skills training for girls, and the importance of female solidarity in defending against abuse. But rural projects such as MORWADAS, as well as NGOs working in the cities to address the needs of ex-combatants, continue to depend on support from the global community to make this vision of human rights a living reality.

Sources:

McKay, S., and Mazurana, D. (2004). *Where Are the Girls? Girls and Fighting Forces in Northern Uganda, Sierra Leone and Mozambique: Their Lives During and After the War.* Montreal, Quebec: Rights & Democracy.

Shepler, S. (2002). Les Filles-soldats: Trajectoires d'Apres-guerre en Sierra Leone [Child Post-war Trajectories for Girls Associated with the Fighting Forces in Sierra Leone]. *Politique Africaine, 21,* 49–62.

Discussing the Reintegration of Child Soldiers

As you watch Part III, "Peace," from *Diamonds, Guns, and Rice: Sierra Leone and the Women's Peace Movement*, respond to the following questions:

1) What issues are there for the children in returning to their communities?

2) What issues arise as obstacles for communities trying to reintegrate child soldiers?

3) What methods are communities and former child soldiers using to overcome obstacles to reintegration?

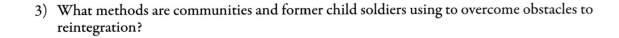

Decision Process Guidelines

The Decision Process Guidelines consist of a four-step process of deciding whether or not to reintegrate former child combatants into their communities. Each step introduces issues that should be considered prior to recommending a course of action.

The first step invites discussion on who holds responsibility for the behavior of child combatants, and how to distribute responsibility for the behavior of the returning youths. The second step asks whether or not the community in which a child was born holds primary responsibility and under what conditions that community should reintegrate the youth. The third step addresses conflicts that may arise in deciding on a plan of action. The fourth step suggests potential courses of action and steps the community could take to put their decision into practice.

Step 1

Where do you think responsibility lies for the actions of former child soldiers? Are children responsible? Are their families responsible? What role has their community played? How is the broader Sierra Leonean society or the international community implicated? Does responsibility lie with a combination of players?

Step 2

Do you believe that the community in which the child was born and raised should accept any responsibility for the problem?

If you decide that the community should accept no responsibility for child combatants, what choices are to be made? For example, exclude former child combatants from returning to the village? Develop emergency plans in case the child does return?

If you decide that the community should accept all responsibility for child combatants, what choices are to be made? For example, should they accept the youth back into the community? How can the community help the child? Who will be in charge of overseeing the child?

Step 3

Provide brief responses to the following questions as considerations in the decision process:

> Who should take responsibility for the welfare of former child combatants (e.g., the community, the government, nongovernmental organizations)?

> To what extent is it the responsibility of child combatants to readjust to their communities as opposed to the responsibility of the community to make allowances for the child soldiers?

> Does the age of the youth make a difference in how the community should respond?

> Does the gender of the youth make a difference in how the community should respond?

Step 4

Create a detailed course of action concerning the reintegration of returning child soldiers based on the decisions of your community. Action plans should draw on responses to the previous questions, your own ideas, and the suggestions listed below.

Refuse to accept any former child combatants back into the community

Subject all former child combatants to legal prosecution

Execute all former combatants, including children

Turn the children over to nongovernmental organizations (NGOs)

Reintegrate all former child combatants unconditionally

Reintegrate all former child combatants conditionally:

> Require former child combatants to complete a trial period in an Interim Care Center before deciding on reintegration.

> Require former child combatants to engage in restitution activities for their communities.

> Require former child combatants to demonstrate their remorse and their desire to return to their communities, e.g., by participating in cultural activities.

Child Soldier A: Fatou Kamera,* Age 14

The time I was captured I was quite young, fourteen years old. My breasts were not yet developed. I was caught with other girls. We were given the choice to join with the rebels or be killed. My parents run away, my aunties run away. I had no choice but to join. We were almost starved. They asked us to cook, but we were little girls and we could not cook. So we were punished. After we had cooked, they gave us the carbons, what is burned from the bottom of the pot. So we had nothing to eat, but we were eating what we were given. Eventually I was forced to have sex with them, and four of them had sex with me in a single night. I almost died. When I was caught, I had never started menstruating. But when I was with them, I was a woman and I started menstruating. That's a long time.

So we were conscripted forcefully. We were given guns and we went out to loot. And we killed people in the villages. I killed five people. After killing the people I started crying, because that was not our wish. If I refused to do certain things I was beaten, raped, and starved for days. So that was our life. We were sent to various villages with guns, and they would force us to go back and kill people. We looted and took all we could find—rice, palm oil, chicken, pots, spoons—we took those things to live in the bush so we would be able to provide food for the whole camp. At times we were too tired to go into battle—the rebels went on their own.

After months with the rebels I was rescued by British soldiers, but every time I remember I get scared. Another thing that bothered me while I was in their hands was that when the rebels captured people, they killed the people, then they threw them in the water. My intention as a girl was to have gone to school. But the schooling I had in the bush with the rebels, I would not call that schooling. They would give me the gun, I would scatter the gun and then assemble the gun again. I knew how to do those things, to use the gun to go out and kill people. Now I want to do tailoring. I have been doing tailoring for one year. And I want a family, a child, later on.

*Fatou (pseudonym) was interviewed at the Moawoma Rural Women's Development Association (MORWODAS) in Sierra Leone. (May 18, 2005). She consented to having her story told to educate others on the effects of war on girls. The interview was conducted in Krio and interpreted by Professor Maude Peacock of the Milton Margai College of Education and Technology, and Elizabeth Bockarie, a staff member at MORWODAS.

Child Soldier B: Abbas Fofanah,* Age 16

I was on my way to the market when a rebel demanded I come with him. The commander said to move ahead with him. My grandmother argued with him. He shot her twice. I said he should kill me too. They tied my elbows behind my back. At the base, they locked me in the toilet for two days. When they let me out, they carved the letters RUF across my chest. They tied me so I wouldn't rub it until it was healed.

They gave me injections in the leg and cut the back of my head to put in the drugs, usually cocaine. The smaller boys stand in front when we fight, the older ones behind. So they give the small boys the injections. It happened anytime we were going on the attack—more than 25 times.

When we caught kamajors (traditional male societies that formed local civil defense groups) we would mutilate them and display them in the streets. When villagers refused to clear out of an area we would strip them naked and burn them to death. Sometimes we used plastic and sometimes a tire. Sometimes they would partially sever a person's neck, then leave him on the road to die slowly. I saw a pregnant woman split open to see what the baby's sex was. We had met her on the streets of Kabala. Two officers, "O5" and "Savage," argued over it and made a bet. Savage's boys opened the woman. It was a girl. The baby lived.

In Kabala I was forced to do amputations. We had a cutlass, an ax and a big log. We called the villagers out and let them stand in line. You ask (the victims) whether they want a long hand or a short hand (the amputation at the wrist or elbow). The long hand you put in a different bag from the short hand. If you have a large number of amputated hands in the bag, the promotion will be automatic, to various ranks.

Sometimes I feel dizzy, and I feel like doing bad things. I go in the house and lie down. Three months ago a friend insulted me, called me a rebel who killed so many people and destroyed the whole world. I said, "You won't make remarks like that again." I met a woman slicing potato leaves. I snatched the knife from her and stabbed him. I ripped his skin. When I see a pretty woman passing I think of the times in the bush when we were raping women, when I could just call her and say, "Come here, let's go." Right now I want to be a doctor or a teacher. I want to go to America to learn a very powerful job. Let me be able to do something for my people.

*Pseudonym

Source:

Masland, T. (2002, May 13). We Beat and Killed People. *Newsweek*, 139, p. 24–30.

Village Elder 1: Alimani Mansaray*

For this exercise, you are a village elder named Alimani Mansaray. You are a 46-year-old man who was headmaster at an elementary school before the civil war. You are deciding if, and under what conditions, child soldiers originally from your village should be integrated back into the community.

This is your story:

The rebels entered the village in the middle of the night. They were going from door to door, pulling people out of their beds into the courtyard, demanding money. I ran into the back garden with my wife and my children. We kept running until we were in the bush. We saw three other people from the village and we huddled together with them. Many of the soldiers we saw were young boys. It is they who did the amputations. We stayed out in the bush for two days, drinking rainwater with nothing to eat.

When we returned to the village we saw that many of the houses had been burned. Ours was still standing but it had been ransacked. Several bodies were lying in the dust. The rebels had taken everything, books, radio, dishes, pots, pans, clothes, food, and all of our life savings. We had no time to hide the money, and all of it was gone.

Many of the villagers were killed or amputated. Others stayed in the bush, out of terror of returning. We heard the crackle of fire nearby. I went to the storehouse, which was not raided, and moved the supplies to the banana plantation. We got some cassavas (root vegetables), picked up some mattresses and retreated back into the bush. It did not seem safe to stay in the village. We took what possessions we could carry and walked to a refugee camp just over the border in Guinea. It was a very long way.

We were able to return when peace was declared and we are just beginning to rebuild our lives from the havoc that the war has brought upon us. Now we are being asked to take former child soldiers back into our village but how can they help us? I know these children but some have been gone for years and have learned rebel ways. They do not take discipline. They are wild. They say that they were abducted, that they were on drugs when they cut off hands and murdered people. The girls have returned with babies. They are ruined and cannot be married. We are being asked to forgive these rebels and let them return but I do not see how we can take them back. They are disrespectful and violent. They have done the unforgivable. These children cannot contribute to the village—they can only take more from us. Let the international community take care of them. Turn them over to a nongovernmental organization, or an Interim Care Center, or prosecute and jail them. I do not care what happens to them. I just never want them back here ever again.

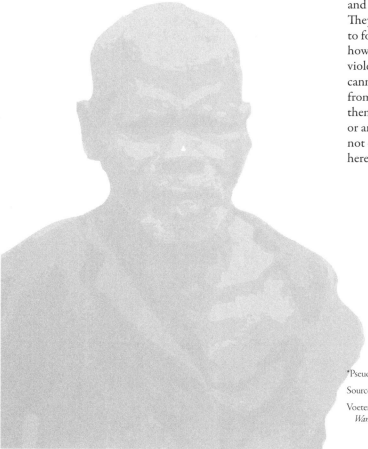

*Pseudonym

Source:

Voeten, Tuen. (2000). *How de Body?: One Man's Terrifying Journey Through an African War.* Amsterdam: Meulenhoff.

Village Elder 2: Tichaona Dumbaya*

For this exercise, you are a village elder named Tichaona Dumbaya. You are a 35-year-old woman who sold rice pap in the village before the civil war. You are considering if, and under what conditions, child soldiers originally from your village should be integrated back into the community.

This is your story:

The rebels entered my village at night and we heard the guns firing. I jumped out of bed and woke up my children. I was going to run to the bush with them but the rebels caught us. They took all our money and the radio. They occupied the village until we harvested crops and then they left with our food. They stole my two eldest children, my son who was eight and my daughter who was fourteen. I did not know what would become of them. I cried and prayed every day for their return.

I was one of the lucky ones because I still have my hands. The rebels asked people if they would like a "long sleeve or a short sleeve." They amputated hands, put the hands in a sack and took them away. They said to tell the president of Sierra Leone that "the future was in our hands." In Sierra Leone you vote by giving a thumbprint at the voting place. Without a hand, you cannot give a thumbprint and therefore you cannot vote.

That was five years ago. Now the children of the village have returned but they are very changed. My son is thirteen and he looks at me with blank eyes. He doesn't listen to me and he gets angry, even violent. I do not know him. I am afraid of him. The other people in the village are angry at him. They say that he is "lost," that he will never be the same, that he has been changed forever. Can nothing be done to bring him back?

My daughter returned with a baby. Now she cannot be married. She will not fetch a bride price because she is no longer virgin. The boys, even those who were with the rebels, say that she is no good, that she is ruined. I do not know what to make of this. The war has been so hard on everyone.

I want my children to come back to me, but I am not sure if this is the best for them or for the community. I do not know what to do. We have an obligation to the children, otherwise they will go back to their rebel ways. If we give them nothing, no shelter, no food, and no guidance, they will be forced to steal what they need to survive. Yet they have been so changed that I am not sure that they can come back and I'm not sure that we have the resources to handle them. With food so scarce, I don't know if we can even feed them, but should we not even try?

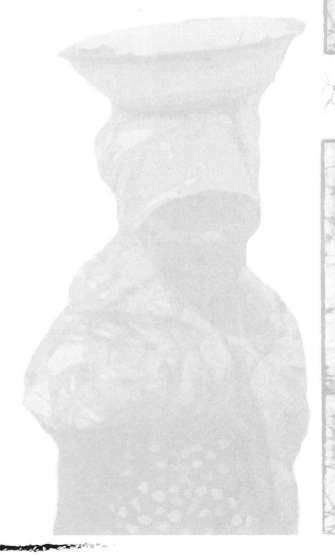

*Pseudonym

Source:

This account is based on oral histories from Sierra Leonean women.

Village Elder 3: Amara Fomba*

For this exercise, you are a village elder named Amara Fomba. You are a 42-year-old woman who worked on a rice plantation. You are considering if, and under what conditions, child soldiers originally from your village should be integrated back into the community.

This is your story:

My daughter was abducted two years ago from our village while she was doing laundry at the river with my mother. They shot my mother and took my daughter into the bush. My sister ran to tell me the news and I went looking for her, but I could not find her. The rebels burned our village so I no longer had a home. I left the village to find food. I walked many miles, and asked many people, but I could not find her. It was very dangerous on the road. I was trying to meet up with the rebels instead of avoiding them, like most people did. I talked to rebel commanders, I went into rebel camps. I made my way north and ended up in Freetown with my sister. I was in Freetown when the rebels invaded, which was a terrible event. I walked to Foreconiah, Guinea with my sister and her children and then on to Kobekora Refugee Camp where I stayed for many months. There I was able to join together with other women to form the Sierra Leonean Peace movement. We women came together to figure out how to find our voices, to work for peace. We have endured so much in this war. We cannot let war happen again.

I came back to my village and began the task of rebuilding. I worked hard. Food was scarce, but I survived. I joined with others to rebuild our houses and the school. I worked with other women to create a women's center. Women are organizing. We have learned a lot from our experiences during the war. We cannot go back to the way things were before, subordinate to our husbands, unable to say what we think. We will take our places beside the men. We have proven how essential we are to the economy and to the government.

I did not hear from my daughter until she came back to the village with her baby. She was weak and ill but I cared for her and her child. I am so grateful that she returned. Now she is in school and at the top of her class. She is doing so well back at home in the community. I take care of her child during the day. I want her to learn new skills, to be able to support herself. We need to help our daughters to find a new voice, a new strength. They say that she cannot be married because she has a baby, because she was with the rebels. I say why is that? And why can she not learn to earn her own living? Why can we not join together to produce goods to sell? Why must a woman be dependent on her husband? My husband is dead. I cannot depend on him. Women, like all Sierra Leoneans, need to come together to find new ways of working and living. If we cannot help each other who can help us? Participation from the outside world seems to only keep us down. Now is the time for communities to come together and take care of one another. If my daughter can come home, so can the other children.

These are our children and they need us now. We need to take them in. They are our future. We cannot afford to turn our backs on them. We cannot afford to throw them away. If we do not take them in, then where will they go? They cannot stay in an Interim Care Center forever. Will they take up arms again and go into the bush? That is not acceptable. It is up to us to give them guidance and hope.

*Pseudonym

Source:

This account is based on oral histories from Sierra Leonean women.

Prosecuting De Beers

You are an attorney prosecuting the De Beers Corporation in front of the International Tribunal. First, you will argue that the De Beers Corporation bears some responsibility for creating the conditions that led to civil war in Sierra Leone. Next, you will recommend rulings. Last, you will respond to questions from the Judges.

To prepare your case read the handout "Blood Diamonds" and respond to the following questions in writing:

> What charges can you bring against the De Beers Corporation, i.e., how did their actions contribute to the conflict in Sierra Leone, and what were those actions?

> What action(s) will you recommend the judges take to bring justice to Sierra Leone and promote reconciliation?

> Are there other players who have not been identified?

The following points are some of the arguments to anticipate from the defense. In your group create a strategy for countering these arguments if introduced by the defense:

> The civil war would have broken out regardless of the diamond trade.

> It was the rebels who mined diamonds illegally and traded them for weapons, not the De Beers Corporation.

> De Beers runs a legitimate business in a competitive environment and pays industry standard wages.

> It is the fault of the Small Arms Manufacturers, who supplied weapons.

Recommendations for possible rulings:

> Which options make sense? Which of these, if any, will you recommend? Do you have other ideas for recommendations for rulings?

>> Ban De Beers from doing business in Sierra Leone.

>> Ban De Beers from participating in the international diamond trade.

>> Levy fines on the De Beers Corporation.

>> Arrest De Beers officials.

>> Require De Beers Corporation to fund education in Sierra Leone.
>> (How would they fund it? By fines or by using a percentage of profits?)

>> Require De Beers Corporation to pay workers a living wage.

Prosecuting Small Arms Manufacturers

You are an attorney prosecuting the Small Arms Manufacturers in front of the International Tribunal. First, you will argue that Small Arms Manufacturers bear some responsibility for creating the conditions that led to civil war in Sierra Leone. Next, you will recommend rulings. Last, you will respond to questions from the Judges.

To prepare your case read the essay "Small Arms: The Real Weapons of Mass Destruction?" and respond to the following questions in writing:

> What charges can you bring against the small arms manufacturer, i.e., how did their actions contribute to the conflict in Sierra Leone and what were those actions?
>
> What action will you recommend the judges take to bring justice to Sierra Leone and promote reconciliation?
>
> Are there other players that have not been identified?

The following points are some of the arguments to anticipate from the defense. In your group, create a strategy for countering these arguments if introduced by the defense:

> Civil war would have happened despite the availability of small arms.
>
> It was rebels who used the guns illegally and not the manufacturers.
>
> There are many manufacturers and it is hard to track the weapons.
>
> Banning weapons from Sierra Leone is impossible unless you ban all weapons everywhere, and people do need some arms for protection.
>
> Manufacturing small arms is a legitimate business that employs many workers—Small Arms Manufacturers have a right to exist.

Recommendations for possible rulings:

> Which options make sense? Which of these, if any, will you recommend? Do you have other ideas for recommendations for rulings?
>
>> Ban the Small Arms Manufacturers from doing business in Sierra Leone.
>>
>> Ban small arms or regulate the international trade more heavily.
>>
>> Levy fines or taxes on the Small Arms Manufacturers.
>>
>> Require Small Arms Manufacturers to redesign guns to be difficult to smuggle, or so that they cannot be used except by the legal buyer, i.e., have legitimate gun dealers mail consumers pin numbers to disable the safety mode on their gun after a sale.
>>
>> Require small arms manufacturers to fund education and rebuild Sierra Leone. (How could they fund it? Use fines or a percentage of profits?)

Defending De Beers

You are an attorney for the De Beers Corporation and have been retained to defend them in front of the International Tribunal. Your job is to develop a line of legal argument to absolve them of responsibility for the deaths associated with the Sierra Leonean civil war. First, you will argue that the De Beers Corporation does not bear any responsibility for creating the conditions that led to civil war in Sierra Leone. Next, you will respond to questions from the Judges.

To prepare your case read the handout "Blood Diamonds" and respond to the following questions in writing:

> What do you think the charges against the De Beers Corporation will be, i.e., what do you think the prosecutors will argue to prove that actions of the De Beers Corporation contributed to the conflict in Sierra Leone, and what were those actions?
>
> What has the De Beers Corporation done to help Sierra Leoneans in the past?
>
> Why is the De Beers Corporation innocent of all charges?
>
> What has the De Beers Corporation done to ensure a "clean" diamond trade?
>
> Are there other parties who are responsible but have not been identified? Can you displace blame onto someone else?

The following points are some arguments to anticipate from the prosecution. In your group, create a strategy for countering these arguments if introduced by the prosecution:

>> De Beers made huge profits while exploiting workers and paying them pennies a day
>>
>> Human rights groups have accused De Beers of buying blood diamonds from rebels in order to maintain control of the diamond industry
>>
>> Diamonds are traded to buy the weapons that fueled the Sierra Leonean civil war
>>
>> Despite the implementation of a plan to certify diamonds as "clean" it is impossible to distinguish between clean and dirty diamonds—certification is easy to forge.

Defending Small Arms Manufacturers

You are the attorney for the Small Arms Manufacturers and have been retained to defend them in front of the International Tribunal. Your job is to develop a line of legal argument to absolve them of responsibility for the deaths associated with the Sierra Leonean civil war. First, you will argue that the Small Arms Manufacturers do not bear any responsibility for creating the conditions that led to civil war in Sierra Leone. Next, you will respond to questions from the Judges.

To prepare your case read the essay "Small Arms: The Real Weapons of Mass Destruction?" and respond to the following questions in writing:

> What do you think the charges against the small arm manufacturers will be, i.e., what do you think the prosecutors will argue to prove that the availability of small arms contributed to the Sierra Leonean civil war?

> Why are Small Arms Manufacturers innocent of all charges?

> What have Small Arms Manufacturers contributed to the fight against the illegal weapons trade?

> Are there other parties who are responsible but have not been identified? Can you displace blame onto someone else?

The following points are some of the arguments to anticipate from the prosecution. In your group, create a strategy for countering these arguments if introduced by the prosecution:

> Small Arms Manufacturers ignore who buys weapons and the consequences of those sales—they sell to rebels and corrupt governments to make more money.

> Small arms are more easily used by child soldiers populating low levels of rebel and government military ranks.

> Besides the machete, small arms were the primary weapon used in the Sierra Leonean civil war and as such helped fuel the conflict.

> Small arms initially bought legally often end up on the black market.

Judging the International Tribunal

Y ou are a Judge on the International Tribunal. The De Beers Corporation and the Small Arms Manufacturers are charged with creating conditions that led to civil war in Sierra Leone. First listen to arguments from prosecutors and defense attorneys representing the two international players. Next ask both sides questions. Last make decisions on guilt and rulings.

To prepare for the De Beers' trial read the handout "Blood Diamonds." To prepare for the Small Arms Manufacturers' trial read the essay "Small Arms: The Real Weapons of Mass Destruction?" Respond to the following questions in writing:

> What charges do you think prosecutors will bring against the De Beers Corporation and the Small Arms Manufacturers? How did each international player contribute to the Sierra Leonean Civil war?

> What questions will you ask Defense Attorneys and Prosecutors for the De Beers Corporation and for the Small Arms Manufacturers?

> How will you determine the degree of responsibility of each player? What are your criteria for guilt or innocence?

Rulings the prosecution may recommend for the De Beers Corporation:

> Ban De Beers from doing business in Sierra Leone.

> Ban De Beers from participating in the international diamond trade.

> Levy fines on the De Beers Corporation.

> Arrest De Beers officials.

> Require De Beers to fund education and rebuild Sierra Leone. (How would they fund it? Use fines or a percentage of profits?)

> Require De Beers Corporation to pay workers a living wage.

Rulings the prosecution may recommend for Small Arms Manufacturers:

> Ban small arms manufacturers from doing business in Sierra Leone

> Ban small arms internationally or regulate small arms internationally

> Levy fines or taxes on the small arms manufacturers

> Require Small Arms Manufacturers to redesign guns to be difficult to smuggle, or so that they cannot be used except by the legal buyer, i.e., have dealers mail consumers pin numbers to disable the safety mode on their gun after a sale

> Require small arms manufacturers to fund education and rebuild Sierra Leone. (How would they fund it? Use fines or a percentage of profits?)

Which options make sense? Which, if any, will you recommend? Do you have other ideas? How will rulings be enforced if adopted?

Blood Diamonds

Established in the early nineteenth century as a colony for escaped slaves, Sierra Leone came under British control in 1896. In 1927 vast diamond deposits were discovered, and by 1932, De Beers, a British based company that originated in South Africa, struck a deal with the Sierra Leonean government giving De Beers sole diamond mining rights for 99 years. In exchange for 27% of net profits, the government nationalized ownership of all diamonds, making them government property. Nationalization in principle creates a form of public ownership over resources. But governments that are not accountable to the people can exploit public ownership for their own interests. The Sierra Leonean government served as a diamond broker for De Beers, with little of the revenue from the mines benefiting the country.

Alluvial and Kimberlite Diamond Deposits

Both alluvial and kimberlite diamond deposits continue to be found in Sierra Leone. Kimberlite deposits are located in volcanic pipes, which originate deep beneath the earth's surface and often require expensive mining equipment. Alluvial diamonds, which break loose from eroded kimberlite pipes, are found close to the earth's surface. These diamonds travel down streams and rivers until they are eventually deposited in mud and thick gravel.

David Keene, professor at the London School of Economics concluded, "Historically most of the profits have accrued abroad. The Alluvial Diamond Mining Scheme set up in 1955 created the possibility of mining by local people, but in practice those who could afford the licenses and the necessary rudimentary equipment were primarily civil servants, chiefs, politicians and most importantly traders." Keene added, "Meanwhile, chiefs in the diamondiferous areas grew rich off the gems, benefiting from their ability to grant licenses and often reserving the best areas for themselves. Ruling house families tended to have ownership in land which they would then lease to others. These licenses were often passed down on a hereditary basis, and ultimate ownership tended to remain with the ruling families, reinforcing their power."

Dirty and Clean Diamonds

"Blood," "dirty," "illicit" and "conflict" are terms used to describe diamonds that are mined and sold illegally. These terms also refer to diamonds traded by rebel movements to finance military activities in opposition to internationally recognized governments. These illegal diamonds are smuggled over borders and often sold for cash or traded for guns. By illegally trafficking diamonds, rebel groups gained control over some of the richest diamond mines in Sierra Leone during the 1990s.

Governments and recognized businesses or corporations legally mine "clean diamonds." In response to public concern that the diamond trade was financing rebel groups in Liberia and Sierra Leone in the 1990s, a political campaign emerged in the United States to control the illegal trafficking in diamonds. In the legal markets, however, diamond mine workers typically labor for pennies a day, while corporate monopolies inflate diamond prices and generate enormous profits from diamonds sales around the world. Since diamonds are extracted for sale in foreign countries, profits are not invested in the development of the country. Although Sierra Leonean workers extract tens of millions of dollars in diamonds each year, the country is ranked as among the world's poorest.

In 1999 human rights groups accused De Beers—the corporation in control of the majority of diamonds worldwide since the early 1900s—of buying blood diamonds from rebels in order to maintain control over the diamond industry. In response, De Beers initiated a campaign to keep blood diamonds out of the world market.

Certificates of Origination

The Kimberly Process, a plan with the goal of establishing worldwide standards for diamond certification, is aimed at preventing conflict diamonds from entering the world market. Under the Kimberly Process plan, diamond-producing countries must issue certificates declaring their diamonds legal and legitimate. Corporations, such as De Beers, have suggested that requiring a certificate of origination for diamonds makes it possible to track diamonds and to prevent rebel groups from using diamonds to finance their activities.

Although over thirty countries have agreed to the certification plan there has not been an independent group formed to monitor diamond production worldwide, or to audit how certificates are issued. How or if they enforce the Kimberly Process is left to each country's government. With no regulation certificates can be easily forged—even rebel groups have been able to successfully apply for and receive legal certification for illicitly traded diamonds.

Where Diamonds are Processed and Cut

Whether diamonds are smuggled over borders or given certificates of legitimacy, it is impossible to distinguish between clean and dirty diamonds once they have entered the world market. Approximately 20% of the world's consumer quality diamonds are processed and cut in Tel Aviv, India and New York City. An estimated 80% of the world's consumer quality diamonds are sent to Antwerp, Belgium, where the majority have been received for over 50 years with no questions asked. In Antwerp legitimate and illicit diamonds are cut and polished, traded and transferred until the difference between clean diamonds and blood diamonds becomes murky. These diamonds, the majority of which are ultimately purchased in US markets, are sold and resold with little or no paperwork.

Sources:

All About Diamonds. (n.d.). Retrieved November 5, 2003, from http://www.goldandsilvermines.com/aboutd.htm

Amnesty International. *The True Cost of Diamonds.* [n.d.]. Retrieved February 4, 2003, from http://web.amnesty.org/pages/ec_kimberley_process

The Belgium Diamond Market. (n.d.). Retrieved April 21, 2005, from Conflict Diamonds: Analyses, Actions, Solutions http://www.conflictdiamonds.com/pages/Interface/reportframe.html

Campbell, G. (2002). *Diamonds: Tracing the Deadly Path of the World's Most Precious Stones.* Boulder, CO: Westview Press.

Cockburn, A. (2002). Diamonds the Real Story. *National Geographic,* March, 6–38.

Doyle, M. (2000). *Call for West Africa Diamond Boycott.* Retrieved August 21, 2001, from http://news.bbc.co.uk/1/hi/world/africa/600475.stm

Epstein, E. & Epstein, J. (1982). *The Rise and Fall of Diamonds.* New York: Simon & Schuster.

Hart, M. (2002). *Diamond: The History of a Cold Blooded Love Affair.* New York: Plume.

Kanfer, S. (1993). *Last Empire: De Beers, Diamonds, and the World.* New York: Farrar Straus Giroux.

Keene, D. (2003). Greedy Elites, Dwindling Resources, Alienated Youths: The Anatomy of Protracted Violence in Sierra Leone. *International Politics and Society, 2.* Retrieved from http://fesportal.fes.de/pls/portal30/docs/FOLDER/IPG/IPG2_2003/ARTKEEN.HTM

Lyden, J., & Montgomery, M. *De Beers and the Diamond Mystique.* Retrieved January 19, 2003, from http://www.americanradioworks.org/features/diamonds/mystique1.html

Supplementary Resources

Web Sites:

Amnesty International. Retrieved June 27, 2005, from http://www.amnesty.org/

> A worldwide movement of people who campaign for internationally recognized human rights. Research and action is focused on preventing and ending grave abuses of the rights to physical and mental integrity, freedom of conscience and expression, and freedom from discrimination, within the context of promoting all human rights

Human Rights Watch—Arms Division. Retrieved June 27, 2005, from http://www.hrw.org/doc/?t=arms

> An independent, nongovernmental organization that investigates and exposes human rights violations, and holds abusers accountable. The organization stands with victims and activists to prevent discrimination, to uphold political freedom, to protect people from inhumane conduct in wartime, and to bring offenders to justice.

iEARN Sierra Leone. Retrieved April 27, 2005, from http://www.iearnsierraleone.org/

> A nongovernmental organization established to serve Sierra Leonean youths who have suffered from war. Programs are designed to directly rehabilitate Sierra Leonean youths by engaging them in creative writing, music, drama, computer skills and literacy, film-making and fine arts, as well as to promote peace education in schools in Sierra Leone and all over the world.

International Action Network on Small Arms. Retrieved April 27, 2005, from http://www.iansa.org/

> A global network of more than 500 civil society organizations working to stop the proliferation and misuse of small arms and light weapons by raising awareness, promoting the work of nongovernmental organizations, fostering collaborative advocacy efforts, establishing regional and subject-specific small arms networks and promoting the voices of victims.

Sierra Leone's Truth and Reconciliation Commission. Retrieved August, 2003, from http://www.sierra-leone.org/trc-documents.html

> Official Web site for the Sierra Leone Truth and Reconciliation Commission, including progress updates, related documents, press briefings, Web links and photographs.

Talking Drum Studio. Retrieved September, 2003, from http://www.sfcg.org/eccg/eccglocdetail.cfm?locus=SL&name=programs&programid=306
> Uses media and outreach to encourage peace and reconciliation. To help find solutions to ongoing and new conflicts in Sierra Leone, the studio participates in peace carnivals, undertakes community radio outreach, and collaborates with government agencies and local and international organizations to promote local, national and sub-regional dialogue.

The Citizens' Network On Essential Services. Retrieved May 3, 2005, from http://www.servicesforall.org/index.shtml

> Works to democratize national and global governance by supporting development of citizens' groups that are engaged in influencing policy decisions about basic services: water, power, education and health care. Demystifies the roles of the World Bank, the International Monetary Fund and World Trade Organization in shaping policies that affect services.

Foreign Policy in Focus. Retrieved July, 2002, from http://www.fpif.org/project-info.html

> A "think tank without walls," that functions as an international network of more than 650 policy analysts and advocates committed to advancing a citizen-based foreign policy agenda—one that is fundamentally rooted in citizen initiatives and movements.

The Independent Media Center. Retrieved, January, 2003, from http://www.indymedia.org/

> A collective of independent media organizations and journalists committed to offering a democratic outlet for the creation of radical, accurate and passionate telling of truth by non-corporate media sources.

International Monetary Fund. Retrieved July, 2002, from http://www.imf.org/

> Includes general reports, country reports, news releases, publications, financial information, projects, policies and history of the International Monetary Fund.

Jubilee USA Network. Retrieved July, 2002, from http://www.jubileeusa.org/start.htm

> Provides useful information and action opportunities for those working to alleviate debts developing nations owe to international financial institutions.

Rethinking Schools: An Urban Educational Journal. Retrieved July, 2002, from http://www.rethinkingschools.org/

> Publishes educational materials that emphasize problems facing urban schools. Publications focus on education and activism as well as key policy issues related to education, with articles written by and for teachers, parents and students.

World Bank. Retrieved July, 2002, from http://www.worldbank.org/

> Includes general reports, country reports, news releases, publications, financial information, projects, policies and history of the World Bank.

Related Publications:

Badri, A. E., & Abdel Sadig, I. I. (1998). *Sudan Between Peace and War: Internationally Displaced Women in Khartoum and South and West Kordofan.* Nairobi, Kenya: United Nations Development Fund for Women.

> A case study of the Sudan introducing perspectives of women on war, conflict resolution and peacebuilding, and how the Sudanese civil war transformed gender roles and the broader society.

Bigelow, B. (1985). *Strangers in Their Own Country: Curriculum Guide on South Africa.* Trenton, NJ: Africa World Press.

> Introduces students and teachers to the lives and struggles of the people of South Africa with stories, poems, role plays, news articles, and historical readings.

Bigelow, B. & Peterson, B. (Eds.). (2002). *Rethinking Globalization: Teaching for Justice in an Unjust World.* Milwaukee, OR: Rethinking Schools Press.

> Introduces students at all age levels to processes of globalization—its historical origins and current impact on societies. Includes background readings, lesson plans, teaching articles, role-plays and simulations, student handouts, interviews, poems, cartoons, annotated resource lists and teaching ideas.

Bigelow, B., Childs, S., Diamond, N., Dickerson, D., & Haaken, J. (2000). *Scarves of Many Colors: Muslim Women and the Veil, a Memorial Curriculum in Honor of the Life and Work of Joan Hawkinson Bohorfoush.* Washington, DC: Teaching for Change.

> Based on an award-winning radio film by the same name produced by Joan Hawkinson Bohorfoush and Dinah Dickerson. The CD and accompanying curriculum engage students in thinking critically about stereotypes of covered Islamic women. The audiotape introduces a range of U.S. and Middle Eastern women who tell stories and offer insight into the changing meanings of the veil.

Boone, S. (1986). *Radiance from the Waters: Ideals of Feminine Beauty in Mende Art*. New Haven, CN: Yale University Press.

> Describes a secret female society that guards and transmits feminine ideals of beauty among the Mende people of Sierra Leone and the roots of these ideals in Sierra Leonean history.

Bryden, M., & Steiner, M. I. (1998). *Somalia between Peace and War: Somali Women on the Eve of the 21st Century*. Nairobi, Kenya: United Nations Development Fund for Women.

> A case study of Somalia focused on the role of women in conflict resolution, peacebuilding, and how civil war both reinforces and transforms gender roles.

Giles, W., & Hyndman, J. (Eds.). (2004). *Sites of Violence: Gender and Conflict Zones*. Berkeley, CA: University of California Press.

> Grew out of a collaboration through the Women in Conflict Zones Network. Sections include 1) feminist approaches to gender and conflict; (2) violence against women in war and postwar times; (3) feminist analyses of international organizations and asylum; and (4) negotiating globalization, security and human displacement.

Hook, D. (Ed.) (2004). *Critical Psychology*. Cape Town, South Africa: UCT Press.

> Introduces critiques of traditional and Western models of psychology and places human mind and behavior in a wider societal context. South Africa serves as the primary source of examples in integrating psychology, history, and politics.

Jackson, M. (1982). *Allegories of the Wilderness: Ethics and Ambiguity in Kuranko Narratives*. Bloomington, IN: Indiana University Press.

> A study of folktales of the Kuranko people of Sierra Leone, including examples of traditional stories and how folk literature relates to everyday struggles for survival.

Hirsch, J. (2001). *Sierra Leone: Diamonds and the Struggle for Democracy*. Boulder, CO: Lynne Rienner Publishers.

> Authored by the US ambassador to Sierra Leone in the mid-1990s. Provides an account of Sierra Leone's decline from a promising colony to a brutalized failed state, and the sequence of historical events that led up to the country's collapse into civil war.

Lee, D. T., Sherman, D., Sweeney, M., & Velazquez, E. *A Curriculum Guide for Moving Mountains: The Story of the Mien*. Portland, OR: Publication Services. (Available from Feather & Fin Productions, P.O. Box 8277, Portland, OR 97282).

> A curriculum guide to accompany Moving Mountains, a film documentary based on the South East Asian culture of the Yiu Lien. The film and documentary explore the history and experiences of this refugee group, including their immigration to the United States, through the eyes of women.

McKay, S., & Mazurana, D. (2001). *Raising Women's Voices for Peacebuilding: Vision, Impact, and Limitations of Media Technologies*. London: International Alert.

> Features case studies of women's uses of media technology for purposes of organizing and development. Focuses specifically on the construction of peace projects and access to and control over contemporary means of communications.

McKay, S., & Mazurana, D. (2004). *Where Are the Girls? Girls and Fighting Forces in Northern Uganda, Sierra Leone and Mozambique: Their Lives During and After the War*. Montreal, Quebec: Rights & Democracy.

> Presents research on the militarization of the lives of girls in Africa, and the roles that girls play in fighting forces. The authors use data from their research in Northern Uganda, Mozambique, and Sierra Leone to demonstrate the range of roles girls play in these three conflict zones and the dilemmas girls face in post-conflict situations.

McMichael, P. (2000). *Development and Social Change: A Global Perspective*. Thousand Oaks, CA: Pine Forge Press.

> Introduces case studies to explore instabilities underlying neoliberal policies of global development, including issues such as the "development project" by third world elites.

Minow, M. (1998). *Between Vengeance and Forgiveness: Facing History after Genocide and Mass Violence*. *Boston*: Beacon Press.

> Examines episodes of mass violence in the twentieth century, war crimes, human rights violations, and the challenges to societies in dealing with the aftermath of collective violence.

Petchesky, R. (2003). *Global Prescriptions: Gendering Health and Human Rights*. London: Zed Books.

> Reviews a decade of women's participation in UN conferences, transnational networks, national advocacy efforts and sexual and reproductive health provision to present a more nuanced analysis of the role of transnational women's groups in setting the international and national agendas for women's health.

Zack-Williams, A. B. (March 2001). Child Soldiers in the Civil War in Sierra Leone. *Review of African Political Economy, 29*(87), 73–82.

> Examines economic factors that contributed to youth involvement in the Sierra Leonean civil war.

Films:

Black, S. (Producer) & Kincaid, J. (Writer of Voice-Over Narration). (2001). *Life and Debt* [Motion picture] (Available from New Yorker Films, 16 West 61st Street, New York NY, 10023)

> Portrays the impact of the World Trade Organization and globalization by addressing international lending, structural adjustment policies and free trade, which are represented in the context of the day-to-day realities of the people whose lives they impact in Jamaica.

Carrier, T. (Director), & South Carolina ETV (Producer). (1991). *Family Across the Sea*. [Motion picture]. (Available from California Newsreel: 149 9th St., #420 San Francisco, CA 94103 (415)621-6196)

> Documents the 1989 homecoming trip made by a delegation of the Gullah people of South Carolina to their homeland of Sierra Leone. Designed for a general viewing audience, this video presents an interesting view of cultural anthropology at work, detecting and documenting the links between the groups.

Insight News Television (Producer) & Samura, S. (Writer/Director). (1999). *Cry Freetown* [Motion picture]. (Available from Insight News Television, The Clock House, 28 Old Town, London, SW4 0LB)

> Provides a unique and harrowing account of the victims of the battle for Freetown, Sierra Leone in January 1999. This film is the original uncut English version and is not suitable for children.

Reid, F. (Director/Producer/Director of Photography), & Hoffmann, D. (Director/Editor). (2000). *Long Nights Journey into Day*. [Motion picture] (Available from Iris Films, 2600 10th Street, Suite 413, Berkeley, CA 94710)

> Documents the progress of several cases of the Truth and Reconciliation Commission in South Africa over two years, exploring issues of forgiveness and reparation.

Reynolds, B. (Producer). (1994). *The Diamond Empire* [Television report]. (Available from PBS: http://www.pbs.org/wgbh/pages/frontline/)

> Report chronicles the Oppenheimers of South Africa gained control of the supply, marketing and pricing of the world's diamonds. Examines how the myth about the scarcity of diamonds was created, and how the inflated value of diamonds has been maintained over the decades.

Toepke, A. (Producer/Director), Serrano, A. (Producer/Director), & Grosvenor, V. (Narrator). (1998). *The Language You Cry In*. [Motion picture] (Available from California Newsreel: 149 9th St., #420 San Francisco, CA 94103 (415) 621-6196)

Tells a scholarly detective story reaching from eighteenth century Sierra Leone to the Gullah people of present-day Georgia, helping to restore the "non-history" imposed on African Americans.

Sources

Adebajo, A. (2002). *Building peace in West Africa: Liberia, Sierra Leone, and Guinea-Bissau.* Boulder, CO: Lynne Rienner Publishers.

Akrinade, B. (2001). International Humanitarian Law and the Conflict in Sierra Leone. *Notre Dame Journal of Law, Ethics and Public Policy, 15*, 391–454.

All About Diamonds. (n.d.). Retrieved November 5, 2003, from
http://www.goldandsilvermines.com/aboutd.htm

Amnesty International. *The True Cost of Diamonds.* [n.d.]. Retrieved February 2003, from
http://web.amnesty.org/pages/ec_kimberley_process

Annan, K. (2001, July 9). Small Arms, Big Problems. Speech before The United Nations Conference on the Illicit Trade in Small Arms and Light Weapons in All Its Aspects.

Anonymous. (2002, Dec. 4). Biggest Terror Threat is Small Arms. *Christian Science Monitor.*

BBC News. (2001, Nov. 21). Child Soldier Asks UN for Help. Retrieved from
http://news.bbc.co.uk/hi/english/world/africa

The Belgium Diamond Market. (n.d.). Retrieved April 21, 2005, from http://www.conflictdiamonds.com/pages/Interface/reportframe.html

Bondi, L. (2002). Disillusioned NGOs Blame the United States for a Weak Agreement. *SAIS Review, 22*(1), 229–233.

Bonner, R. (1998, July 13). 21 Nations Seek to Limit the traffic in Small Arms. *The New York Times*, pp. A3.

Campbell, G. (2002). *Diamonds: Tracing the Deadly Path of the World's Most Precious Stones.* Boulder, CO: West View Press.

Christie, D. J., Wagner, R. V., & Winter, D. D. (2001). *Peace, Conflict, and Violence: Peace Psychology for the 21st Century.* Upper Saddle River, NJ: Prentice Hall.

Cockburn, A. (2002). Diamonds the Real Story. *National Geographic,* March, 6–38.

Cook, R. (2001, March 20). Regulating and Reducing the Scourge of Small Arms. *The Independent* (Bangladesh).

Doyle, M. (2000). *Call for West Africa Diamond Boycott.* Retrieved August 21, 2001, from
http://news.bbc.co.uk/1/hi/world/africa/600475.stm

Editorial desk. (2001, July 11). An American Retreat on Small Arms. *The New York Times*, pp. A16.

Enloe, C. (2000). *Bananas, Beaches and Bases: Making Feminist Sense of International Politics.* Berkeley: University of Berkeley Press.

Epstein, E., & Epstein, J. (1982). *The Rise and Fall of Diamonds: The Shattering of a Brilliant Illusion.* New York: Simon & Schuster.

Fanon, F. (1986; 1952). *Black Skin, White Masks.* London: Pluto.

_____(1990; 1963). *The Wretched of the Earth.* London: Penguin.

Farr, K. (2004). *Sex Trafficking: The Global Marketing of Women and Children.* New York: Worth Publishers.

Ferme, M. C. (2001). *The Underneath of Things: Violence, History, and the Everyday in Sierra Leone.* Berkeley, CA: University of California Press.

Fleshman, M. (2001). Small Arms in Africa: Counting the Cost of Gun Violence. *Africa Recovery, 15*(4).

Giles, W. & Hyndman, J. (2004). *Sites of Violence: Gender and Conflict Zones.* Berkeley: University of Berkeley Press.

Haaken, J. (1998). *Pillar of Salt: Gender, Memory and the Perils of Looking Back.* New Brunswick: Rutgers University Press

Haaken, J. (2002, Autumn). Cultural Amnesia: Memory, Trauma and War. Signs: Journal of Women in Culture and Society, 28(1), pp. 455–457

Haaken, J. (2002). The Good, the Bad, and the Ugly: Psychoanalytic and Cultural Perspectives on Forgiveness. In S. Lamb and J.G. Murphy (Eds.). *Before Forgiving: Cautionary Views of Forgiveness in Psychotherapy.* New York: Oxford University Press, pp. 172–191.

Haaken, J. (2002). Stories of Survival: Class, Race, and Domestic Violence. In Nancy Holmstrom (Ed.). *The Socialist Feminist Project: A Contemporary Reader in Theory and Politics.* New York: Monthly Review Press, pp. 102–120

Haaken, J. (2003). Traumatic Revisions: Remembering Abuse and the Politics of Forgiveness. In P. Reavey and S. Warner (Eds.). *New Feminist Stories of Child Sex Abuse.* New York: Routledge, pp. 77–93.

Haaken, J. (Co-producer), & Heymann, C. (Co-producer). (2000). *Diamonds, Guns, and Rice: Sierra Leone and the Women's Peace Movement* [Motion picture]. (Available from Portland State University, Psychology Department, Post Office Box 751, Portland, Oregon, 97207)

Hamber, B. (2004). *Amicus Brief in Support of Khulumani's Lawsuit.* Retrieved July 2005 from Brandon Hamber's Web site: http://www.brandonhamber.com/documents/legalaction-press3.htm

Hart, M. (2002). *Diamond: The History of a Cold-blooded Love Affair.* New York: Plume.

Human Development Report. (1998). Retrieved April 27, 2005, from United Nations Development Program Web site: http://hdr.undp.org/reports/global/1998/en/

Human Rights Watch. (2000, January 17). *United States Opposition Jeopardizes Global Ban on Child Soldiers. Children's Rights*: HRW World Report 2000. Retrieved from http://www.hrw.org/press/2000

Kanfer, S. (1993). *Last Empire: De Beers, Diamonds, and the World.* New York: Farrar Straus Giroux.

Keene, D. (2003). Greedy Elites, Dwindling Resources, Alienated Youths: The Anatomy of Protracted Violence in Sierra Leone. *International Politics and Society, 2.* Retrieved July 2005 from http://fesportal.fes.de/pls/portal30/docs/FOLDER/IPG/IPG2_2003/ARTKEEN.HTM

Klare, M. (1995). Stemming the Lethal Trade in Small Arms and Light Weapons. *Issues in Science and Technology.*

Klare, M. (1999). The Kalashnikov Age. *Bulletin of the Atomic Scientists, 55*(1).

Lyden, J., & Montgomery, M. De Beers and the Diamond Mystique. Retrieved January 2003, from http://www.americanradioworks.org/features/diamonds/mystique1.html

Masland, T. (2002, May 13). We Beat and Killed People. *Newsweek, 139,* 24–30.

McKay, S., & Mazurana, D. (2004). *Where Are the Girls? Girls and Fighting Forces in Northern Uganda, Sierra Leone and Mozambique: Their Lives During and After the War.* Montreal, Quebec: Rights & Democracy.

Pratt, D. (1999). *Sierra Leone: The Forgotten Crisis.* Retrieved from
http://www.sierra-leone.org/pratt042399.html

Rashid, I. (1999). "Do Dady nor Lef me Make dem Carry me": Slave resistance and emancipation in Sierra Leone, 1894–1928. In Susanne Miers and Martin Klein (Eds.). *Slavery and Colonial Rule in Africa.* Portland, OR: Frank Cass, 208–231.

Renner, M. (1999). Arms Control Orphans. *Bulletin of the Atomic Scientists*, 55(1).

Richards, P. (1996). *Fighting for the Rain Forest: War, Youth and Resources in Sierra Leone.* London: International African Institute.

Rosen, D. (1983). The Peasant Context of Feminist Revolt in West Africa. *Anthropological Quarterly*, 56(1), 35–43.

Schocken, C. (2002). *The Special Court for Sierra Leone: Overview and Recommendations.* Retrieved from http://www.law.berkeley.edu/faculty/ddcaron/Public_Website/Courses/Intl%20cts/Seminar%20Fall%202002001/2001-Schocken-on-Sierra-Leone.htm

Shaw, R. (2002). *Memories of the Slave Trade: Ritual and Historical Imagination in Sierra Leone.* Chicago: University of Chicago Press.

Shepler, S. (2002). Les Filles-soldats: Trajectoires d'Apres-guerre en Sierra Leone [Child Post-war Trajectories for Girls Associated with the Fighting Forces in Sierra Leone]. *Politique Africaine*, 21, 49–62.

Sierra Leone Truth and Reconciliation Commission. (2004, October). Sierra Leone Truth and Reconciliation Commission. Overview, Chapter 2, and Chapter 3 retrieved July 2005, from United States Institute of Peace Web site: http://www.usip.org/library/tc/tc_regions/tc_sl.html#rep

The Special Court for Sierra Leone. *The Special Court for Sierra Leone: Basic Facts.* Retrieved from
http://www.sc-sl.org/index.html

Voeten, T. (2000). *How de Body?: One Man's Terrifying Journey Through an African War.* Amsterdam: Meulenhoff.

Ooligan Press

Ooligan Press takes its name from a Native American word for the common smelt or candlefish, a source of wealth for millennia on the Northwest Coast and origin of the word "Oregon." Ooligan is a general trade press rooted in the rich literary life of Portland and the Pacific Northwest. Founded in 2001, it is also a teaching press in the Department of English at Portland State University. Besides publishing books that honor cultural and natural diversity, it is dedicated to teaching the art and craft of publishing. The press is staffed by students pursuing master's degrees in an apprenticeship program under the guidance of a core faculty of publishing professionals. By publishing real books in real markets, students combine theory with practice; the press and the classroom become one.

The following Book Publishing Program students and faculty were instrumental in the creation of *Speaking Out: Women, War, and the Global Economy*.

Susan Applegate
Bernadette Baker
Lake Boggan
Laura Daye
Paulette Rees-Denis
Karen Kirtley and the Advanced Book Editing Students
Gretchen Stelter
Jonah E.R. Loeb
Christopher Ross
Gretchen Stelter
Dennis Stovall

Colophon

Speaking Out: Women, War, and the Global Economy was typographically set in Adobe™ Garamond Premier Pro, Adobe™ Big Caslon, ITC™ Franklin Gothic, and Bodini Standard Poster Compressed using Adobe™ InDesign CS2 and Macintosh™ computers. Watermarks were rendered in Adobe™ Illustrator and Adobe™ Photoshop.

Printed at Central Plains Book Manufacturing, Winfield, Kansas.